MAX notes

Charles Dickens'

Great Expectations

Text by
Judy Clamon
(M.A., East Texas State University)
English Department
Mabank High School
Mabank, Texas

Illustrations by
Karen Pica

 Research & Education Association

MAXnotes™ for
GREAT EXPECTATIONS

Printed in the United States of America

Library of Congress Catalog Card Number 94-65961

International Standard Book Number 0-87891-954-6

MAXnotes™ is a trademark of
Research & Education Association, Piscataway, New Jersey 08854

What **MAXnotes**™ *Will Do for You*

This book is intended to help you absorb the essential contents and features of Charles Dickens' *Great Expectations* and to help you gain a thorough understanding of the work. The book has been designed to do this more quickly and effectively than any other study guide.

For best results, this **MAXnotes** book should be used as a companion to the actual work, not instead of it. The interaction between the two will greatly benefit you.

To help you in your studies, this book presents the most up-to-date interpretations of every section of the actual work, followed by questions and fully explained answers that will enable you to analyze the material critically. The questions also will help you to test your understanding of the work and will prepare you for discussions and exams.

Meaningful illustrations are included to further enhance your understanding and enjoyment of the literary work. The illustrations are designed to place you into the mood and spirit of the work's settings.

The **MAXnotes** also include summaries, character lists, explanations of plot, and chapter-by-chapter analyses. A biography of the author and discussion of the work's historical context will help you put this literary piece into the proper perspective of what is taking place.

The use of this study guide will save you the hours of preparation time that would ordinarily be required to arrive at a complete grasp of this work of literature. You will be well-prepared for classroom discussions, homework, and exams. The guidelines that are included for writing papers and reports on various topics will prepare you for any added work which may be assigned.

The **MAXnotes** will take your grades "to the max."

Dr. Max Fogiel
Program Director

Contents

> **Each chapter includes List of Characters,
> Summary, Analysis, Study Questions and
> Answers, and Suggested Essay Topics.**

Introduction

The Life and Work of Charles Dickens

One of the best-known and most successful English novelists of the nineteenth and twentieth centuries was Charles Dickens. He was born in 1812 at Portsmouth to middle-class parents; yet, as a boy Dickens knew poverty and social disgrace. His father was sent to prison for debt when Dickens was only 12 years of age. The custom at this time required the debtor's wife to accompany her husband to prison along with the younger children. Dickens was the second eldest of eight children and was thus sent to work in a shoe polish warehouse pasting labels on blackening bottles for six shillings a week. He was permitted to visit his family only on Sunday in the Marshalsea Prison. The people and incidents involved in this dark period of Dickens' life appeared in many of his writings. He records much of his own early life in *David Copperfield* and *Great Expectations*. The separation from his family and the unhappiness of his childhood left him with deep feelings of humiliation, loneliness, and rejection which he later expressed through the children of his novels. It was during his early years that his hatred of social injustice and his sympathy for society's outcasts was formed.

Later in his life, Dickens worked as a legal clerk and then a legal shorthand reporter. He married Catherine Hogarth in 1836, and they had 10 children. In 1858, they separated and a young actress, Ellen Lawless Ternan, apparently became his mistress.

Pickwick Papers was Dickens' first major work. Encouraged by its success, he continued to publish most of the rest of his novels serially. *Great Expectations* first appeared in *All the Year Round* in 1860-61 as a serial. Because he was writing in a serial form, this method of writing affected the way Dickens conceived and constructed his plots. He was an expert at weaving the plots so that something exciting was about to happen at the end of each chapter.

In 1842, he visited America and aroused anger by his frank comments about slavery and other social injustices. He began to tour the world giving dramatic readings from his works. Partly from the strain of these public readings, he died in 1870. He is buried in the Poets' Corner of Westminster Abbey.

Dickens wrote 14 novels as well as many shorter works. His novels not only have exciting and memorable plots, but they are also angry exposures of social and moral injustices. Dickens took a marked interest in the social problems of his time, and he attacked injustice wherever he found it.

Historical Background

In order to understand the literature during the Victorian Age, one needs to have an understanding of England at that time. The era is named for England's popular Queen Victoria who ruled for nearly 60 years. This era was a complex time and one of change. It was during the nineteenth century that England definitely became the Great Britain that is known today. The expansion of the British Empire was indeed worldwide. England was wealthy, yet democracy was slowly being forced upon her by industrial changes and political reforms. The problems of a growing democratic spirit in politics and the problems of social and industrial adjustment needed to be solved.

The Industrial Revolution changed England from a primarily agricultural nation to one that was primarily industrial and mercantile. Inventions such as the steam engine, the spinning jenny, and the power loom made machines replace hand labor, giving rise to mass unemployment. The factory system was introduced, and it was in this setting that Dickens grew up. London was the center of world dominance, but raw sewage flowed along its streets. Slums lined the Thames River. Employers used women and child labor at starvation wages. Children were taken from homes of greedy parents or from orphanages and "workhouses" and put to work in the factories.

Along with the Industrial Revolution, there was another revolution taking place between science and theology. Charles Darwin and Thomas Henry Huxley were upsetting the nation with their new doctrine that man evolved from earlier forms through a process of long development. Warfare began between those who believed that Man was created in a day in the image of God and given authority over the animal world, and those who believed Man evolved scientifically.

Victorian literature was another revolution, replacing the romantic literature of the past that had romanticized the upper classes. Victorian literature was written for the people. Magazines became very popular with the English people and catered to all classes of readers. The popular magazines provided an outlet for many writers who wrote their novels in month to month sections, much like a serial. Because these installments usually appeared month to month or week to week, the writer strung his story out based on its popularity with readers. The pressure of social problems tended to create a new awareness of and interest in human beings and relationships; thus, characterization became a dominant quality in literature.

Master List of Characters

Pip (a.k.a. Philip Pirrip, Handel)—*Narrator of the novel who has great expectations.*

Miss Havisham—*Eccentric woman who lives in seclusion after being jilted on her wedding day. She has an adopted daughter Estella.*

Abel Magwitch (a.k.a. Provis, First Convict, Mr. Campbell)—*Pip's benefactor and Estella's father.*

Estella—*Adopted daughter of Miss Havisham who marries Bentley Drummle.*

Joe Gargery—*Married Pip's sister. He is a blacksmith in the village.*

Mrs. Joe Gargery (a.k.a. Georgiana M'Ria)—*Pip's sister who dies as a result of a blow on the head.*

Biddy—*Mr. Wopsle's great-aunt's granddaughter and an orphan. She marries Joe Gargery after the death of Mrs. Joe.*

Mr. Jaggers—*Pip's guardian and Miss Havisham's lawyer. He is also Abel Magwitch's lawyer.*

Herbert Pocket, Pale Young Gentleman—*Pip's roommate in London and close friend.*

John Wemmick—*A clerk in Mr. Jaggers' office.*

Matthew Pocket—*Father to Herbert Pocket and tutor for Pip while he is in London.*

Compeyson, Second Convict—*Fiance who jilted Miss Havisham and partner with Abel Magwitch and Arthur in illegal dealings.*

Uncle Pumblechook—*Joe's uncle and the one who takes the credit for Pip's fortunes.*

Dolge Orlick—*Responsible for Mrs. Joe's death and is Pip's enemy.*

Clara—*Marries Herbert Pocket.*

Bentley Drummle—*Also known as the Spider. Was tutored by Matthew Pocket and married Estella.*

Aged Parent—*John Wemmick's father who is deaf.*

Miss Skiffins—*Marries John Wemmick.*

Molly—*Servant to Mr. Jaggers and Estella's mother.*

Arthur—*Miss Havisham's half brother and a partner to Compeyson.*

Mr. Wopsle, Mr. Waldengarver—*A clerk in the church before becoming an actor.*

Mr. Trabb—*A local tailor and undertaker in Pip's village.*

Mr. Trabb's boy—*Makes fun of Pip when he receives his fortune, but leads Herbert and Startop to the sluice house where Orlick is holding Pip captive.*

Bill Barley, Gruffandgrim—*Father of Clara and an ex-purser.*

Startop—*Like Pip and Drummle, is tutored by Matthew Pocket.*

He is also a friend of Pip's who helps try to get Magwitch out of the country.

Mr. Hubble—*A wheelwright in Pip's village and a guest at Christmas dinner when Pip was young.*

Mrs. Hubble—*Wife of Mr. Hubble and also a guest at Christmas dinner.*

Mr. Wopsle's Great-Aunt—*Runs an evening school in the village. She also runs a little store where Biddy works.*

Mrs. Camilla—*Relative to Miss Havisham.*

Cousin Raymond—*Relative to Miss Havisham.*

Sarah Pocket—*Relative to Miss Havisham and works briefly for her.*

Georgiana Pocket—*Relative to Miss Havisham.*

Mrs. Whimple—*The landlady where Clara and her father live. It is also her house where Magwitch is hidden.*

Flopson and Millers—*Nurses who work for Matthew Pocket.*

Pepper, Avenger—*A servant for Pip while he is in London.*

Skiffins—*Miss Skiffins' brother. He is an accountant who arranges for Herbert to become a partner with Clarriker.*

Clarriker—*The merchant that Pip arranges for Herbert to go into business with.*

Mrs. Brandley—*A widow and the lady Estella is living with in Richmond.*

Belinda Pocket—*Wife of Matthew Pocket and mother to Herbert Pocket.*

Jack—*The man who dresses in the clothes left by roomers or takes them from drowned victims. He is at the public house where Herbert, Magwitch, Pip, and Startop spend the night before rowing out to sea.*

Squires—*Landlord of the Blue Boar.*

Mrs. Coiler—*A widow and a neighbor to Mr. and Mrs. Matthew Pocket.*

Sophia—*A servant of Matthew and Belinda Pocket.*

Colonel—*A soldier in Newgate Prison who is sentenced to die.*

Sally—*Compeyson's wife.*

Mary Anne—*A young servant working for Mr. Wemmick.*

Stranger at the Three Jolly Bargemen—*A recent convict who knew Abel Magwitch. He gave Pip some money from Magwitch and stirred his drink with Joe's file.*

Summary of the Novel

Great Expectations can be divided into three stages in the life of Pip. The first stage presents Pip as an orphan being raised by an unkind sister who resents him, and her husband, who offers him kindness and love. While visiting the tombstones of his parents in the cemetery, Pip encounters a convict and is made to bring him food and a file the next day. Pip's convict and a second convict are caught by soldiers of the Crown and returned to the prison ships (the Hulks).

Uncle Pumblechook arranges for Pip to go to Miss Havisham's house to play, and there he meets and falls in love with Estella. Pip returns to Miss Havisham's house to walk her around the decayed banquet table every other day for nearly 10 months. Miss Havisham rewards Pip for his service by paying for his apprenticeship to become a blacksmith with Joe.

Pip is unhappy with his position and longs to become a gentleman in order that he may eventually win Estella's affection. One day a lawyer, Mr. Jaggers, comes to tell Pip that a beneficiary has left him great fortunes. Pip is to go to London to become a gentleman. Pip believes that the benefactor is Miss Havisham.

The second stage of Pip's life takes place in London where he becomes friends with Herbert Pocket. The two young men live beyond their means and fall deeply in debt. Pip makes friends with Mr. Jaggers' clerk, Mr. Wemmick, and enjoys visiting him at his Castle. Pip is told the background of Miss Havisham and her ill-fated wedding day. He also is embarrassed by a visit from Joe. An unexpected visit from his convict reveals that the convict, not Miss Havisham, is his benefactor. The man's name is Magwitch; he is the one to whom Pip had brought food in the churchyard. This knowledge begins the change in Pip from ungrateful snobbery to the humility associated with Joe and home.

The third stage in Pip's life solves all the remaining mysteries of the novel. Compeyson, the second convict who was Magwitch's enemy, is drowned when Pip tries to aid Magwitch in his escape from London. Pip finds out who Estella's mother and father are. Pip is rescued from Orlick. Magwitch dies in prison, and Pip becomes a clerk in Cairo with Herbert. He returns 11 years later and finds Estella at the site of Satis House. The more popular ending indicated that they stayed together.

Estimated Reading Time

Four weeks should be allowed for the study of *Great Expectations*. Three weeks will be required to read the novel, reading four chapters at a sitting. The student should read every day from Monday through Friday. After reading the chapters, the student should answer all study questions in this book to ensure understanding and comprehension. The essay questions may be used if needed. The fourth week is set aside for reports, projects, and testing as deemed necessary by the teacher.

SECTION TWO

Great Expectations
Part I

Chapter 1

New Characters:

Pip (Philip Pirrip): *a young boy about six or seven years of age who is the narrator of the novel*

Mrs. Joe Gargery: *Pip's sister*

First Convict: *a man who is hiding in the cemetery and threatens to kill Pip by cutting out his heart and liver if he does not bring him "wittles" (food) and a file*

"Philip Pirrip, Late Of This Parish": *inscription written on Pip's father's tombstone*

"Georgiana Wife Of The Above": *inscription written on Pip's mother's tombstone*

Alexander, Bartholomew, Abraham, Tobias, Roger: *Pip's brothers who died as infants; their tombstones are located next to the parents' stones in the cemetery*

Summary

Pip, an orphan being brought up by his sister, goes to the village cemetery to visit the tombstones of his parents and five little brothers. In the churchyard, a convict with an iron on his leg fright-

ens Pip. The escaped convict—wet, cold, and hungry—questions Pip. After learning that Pip lives with his sister and her husband, the convict demands that Pip bring him "wittles" (food) and a file for his leg iron. The convict threatens to cut out Pip's heart and liver if he does not return by the next morning. The demands are enforced with references to an unseen, evil companion who knows how to "get" young boys who do not do as they are told. Pip, terrified, runs home, which is located near the marsh country and 20 miles from the sea.

Analysis

The opening chapter of *Great Expectations* focuses on a young orphan who is visiting his family in the churchyard. Because Pip has no living family, except for his sister with whom he lives, the reader is made to feel sympathy for the young boy. He seems to have a lonely life that is further complicated by the appearance of a convict who threatens him. The convict is also represented as a lonely outsider to society. Loneliness is not only presented in the character of Pip, but also in the setting. The churchyard is presented as dreary, isolated, and overgrown with nettles.

Pip, in Chapter 1, can be described as a young, lonely, and trusting character. He always refers to the convict as "sir." The convict, on the other hand, is coarse in speech and actions. He has obviously escaped from prison and is hiding in the churchyard.

The novel is written from a first person point of view. The story is told from a mature Pip who is looking back over his life and telling his story to the readers, beginning when he was about six or seven years of age.

Study Questions

1. The novel is written in what point of view?
2. Where does the opening scene take place?
3. What is Pip's full name?
4. Where are Pip's parents?
5. With whom does Pip live?
6. What does Joe Gargery do for a living?

7. How is the first convict dressed? What is his appearance?

8. What does the first convict ask Pip to bring him?

9. Why did the first convict ask for a file?

10. Where is Pip to bring the food and the file the next morning?

Answers

1. The novel is written in first person point of view.

2. The opening scene takes place in a churchyard (cemetery).

3. Pip's full name is Philip Pirrip.

4. Pip's parents are buried in the cemetery.

5. Pip lives with his sister and her husband.

6. Joe Gargery is a blacksmith.

7. The first convict is dressed in gray with an iron around his leg, no hat, broken shoes, and an old rag tied around his head. He is soaked with water and covered with mud.

8. The first convict asks Pip to bring him food and a file.

9. The convict plans to file off his leg iron.

10. Pip is to bring the food and the file to the old battery which is a deserted military fortification that used to be equipped with guns.

Suggested Essay Topics

1. Why is the first chapter so important?

2. Compare and contrast Pip and the first convict.

3. What examples of humor can be found in the first chapter?

4. Explain why the story is more interesting written in first person point of view.

Chapters 2 and 3

New Characters:

Joe Gargery: *a blacksmith who is married to Pip's sister*

Second Convict: *an escaped convict from the hulks who has a bruise on his left cheek*

Summary

Pip runs home from the churchyard only to be informed by Joe that his sister is out looking for him. His sister is 20 years older than Pip and is described as "not a good-looking woman...with black hair and eyes and a prevailing redness of skin." Joe, on the other hand, is gentle and protective towards Pip and is described as "a fair man, with curls of flaxen hair on each side of his smooth face." Mrs. Joe returns to the house, and upon finding Pip there, throws him across the room, striking him with "Tickler" (a beating rod). After demanding to know where he has been, she serves Joe and Pip some bread and butter. Remembering his promise to the convict, Pip decides to hide his serving of food down his pants leg. When Pip is sent to bed, he struggles with his fear of the convict's companion and a heavy load of guilt, knowing that in the morning he is going to steal from Mrs. Joe.

Pip gets up at sunrise, steals food, brandy, a pork pie, and one of Joe's files. He then heads for the battery near the churchyard. As he nears the battery, Pip sees a convict huddled with his arms folded in sleep. Pip taps him on the shoulder, but when the startled convict turns around, it is not the first convict. The second convict strikes at Pip and runs off into the mist. Pip proceeds to the battery and locates the first convict, giving him the food and file. Pip asks the convict why he isn't going to share with his companion. The first convict is startled when Pip tells about the second convict with the bruise on his left cheek. The first convict asks Pip which way he ran and begins to rapidly file off his leg iron. Pip hurries home.

Analysis

The feeling of guilt has an unsettling effect on Pip. He cannot sleep; he cannot think of anything but his promise to steal for the convict.

The theme of right and wrong or good and evil is introduced in these chapters. The guilt Pip feels is kept within himself, and he does not seek help or advice from his sister or Joe. Pip's feeling of guilt is further emphasized when he questions his sister about the cannon fire and the Hulks. His sister replies that "people are put in the Hulks because they murder, and because they rob, and forge, and do all sorts of bad; and they always begin by asking questions." Pip firmly believes that he is definitely on his way to join the convicts on the Hulks because he asks questions; even worse, in the morning he is planning to steal.

In Chapters 2 and 3, Dickens presents vivid characterizations of Pip, Joe, and Mrs. Joe. Joe is portrayed as a gentle, caring, but simple man who tries to protect Pip from his sister's wrath. His sister, on the other hand, is the domineering force in the Gargery household. She rules not only Pip, but also Joe, with a firm hand. At this point in Pip's life, he feels that Joe is his friend and equal. Pip, even though he is terrified of the convict, is concerned about the man's health and welfare. More because of his terror than his concern, he does not intend to break his promise.

Study Questions

1. When Pip returns from the churchyard, where is Mrs. Joe?

2. How many times has Mrs. Joe been out looking for Pip?

3. What does Pip mean when he says he was "brought up by hand"?

4. What is the Tickler?

5. Where does Pip hide his bread?

6. What does Mrs. Joe give Pip when she thinks he has eaten his bread too fast?

7. How are the people on shore warned when a convict has escaped from the Hulks?

8. What are the Hulks?

9. What is unusual about the second convict's face?

10.   Who does Pip think the second convict is?

Answers

1.   Mrs. Joe is out looking for Pip.

2.   She has been out 13 times looking for him.

3.   This phrase is an example of a pun, a play on words. The phrase could mean that he is being brought up in the watchful care of his sister. It could also mean that Pip is being brought up with many slaps and spankings from Mrs. Joe.

4.   Tickler is a cane used by Mrs. Joe to discipline Pip.

5.   Pip hides his bread down his pants leg.

6.   Mrs. Joe makes Pip drink a pint of tar-water.

7.   When a convict escapes from the Hulks, people on shore are warned by a cannon firing.

8.   The Hulks are old ships used as a prison for convicts.

9.   The second convict has a badly bruised left cheek.

10.   Pip thinks that the second convict is the mysterious companion of the first convict.

Suggested Essay Topics

1.   Explain how guilt has affected Pip's life.

2.   Define pun, and how it is used in these chapters.

3.   Discuss the theme of right and wrong or good and evil.

4.   How is the relationship between Pip and his sister different from the relationship between Pip and Joe.

Chapters 4 and 5

New Characters:

Mr. Wopsle: *the clerk at church and a guest at the Gargery's Christmas dinner*

Mr. Hubble: *the wheelwright (one who makes and repairs wheels) and a guest at the Gargery's Christmas dinner*

Mrs. Hubble: *wife of the wheelwright, also a guest at the Gargery's*

Uncle Pumblechook: *Joe's uncle, a well-to-do corn chandler (grain merchant) and a guest at the Gargery's*

Sergeant and His Soldiers: *men in pursuit of the two escaped convicts; they stop at the Gargery house to have some handcuffs repaired*

Summary

As the chapter opens, Mrs. Joe is busily cleaning and getting ready for the holiday dinner while Joe and Pip try to stay out of her way. It is Christmas Day, and Pip and Joe go to church where Pip feels the urge to confess his wrongdoing, but he does not. After church the dinner guests arrive, and Pip is constantly in fear that the theft will be discovered. During the dinner, Pip is often compared to a swine and reminded by the dinner guests that he should be grateful to his sister for his upbringing. Mrs. Joe reaches for the stone bottle that holds the brandy and prepares to pour Mr. Pumblechook a drink. After a drink of the liquid, Mr. Pumblechook jumps to his feet and rushes out the door, "violently plunging and expectorating." (Unknowingly, Pip had replaced the stolen brandy with tar-water.) Puzzled about how the tar-water got into the brandy bottle, Mrs. Joe prepares a hot gin and water for Uncle Pumblechook. Finally, Mrs. Joe offers to serve the pork pie, and Pip grabs the table leg to stop his trembling. Mrs. Joe goes to the pantry to get the pork pie which is more than Pip can stand. He runs for the door and runs head-on into a party of soldiers. Pip is certain they have come to arrest him for stealing, because the sergeant is holding a pair of handcuffs. Actually, the sergeant is seeking a blacksmith to have him repair the handcuffs. The soldiers are after the two escaped convicts.

After the cuffs are repaired, Mr. Wopsle, Joe, and Pip join the soldiers in their search for the convicts. Pip, sitting on Joe's back in the sleeting weather, hopes that they do not succeed. He worries that the convict will think that he is the one who brought the soldiers to the marshes. After hearing shouts, the convicts are located in a ditch fighting one another. After capture, the second convict claims that the first convict tried to murder him. The first convict claims that he could have murdered him but preferred to help the soldiers return him to the Hulks. The first convict sees Pip in the group, and Pip quickly shakes his head. Before being returned to the Hulks, the first convict confesses that he was the one who stole from Joe and Mrs. Joe. Joe reassures the convict that they would not want him to starve, no matter what he had done.

Analysis

Throughout the novel, Dickens presents several themes. One of these is the theme of good versus evil. Pip knows that stealing is wrong and that his wrongdoing will more than likely cause him to end up in the Hulks. When Pip and Joe attend church before the Christmas dinner, Pip comes close to confessing. Guilt has consumed the small boy, and he states that what "I suffered outside was nothing to what I underwent within." It is the fear of Mrs. Joe and the knowledge that she would find him guilty of his childhood crimes that causes Pip so much inward pain. Although Pip feels remorse over his actions, he cannot undo any part of it. Pip is caught between his fear of his sister and his fear of the convict. Pip not only feels the guilt of his sins, but is also terrified when he witnesses the capture of the convicts for fear that the first convict will think that Pip betrayed him.

After the convicts are caught, the arguing between the two reveals a small insight into the past lives of both of them. The first convict assures the soldiers that he would rather be caught again than to let the second convict get his freedom. The first convict makes the statement, "Let him make a tool of me afresh and again? Once more? No, no, no." By this statement the reader can assume that the two convicts had known one another before their capture, and in some way, the second convict had taken advantage of the first. There seems to be a tremendous amount of hate between the two.

At the end of Chapter 5, Joe's genuine goodness is seen again as he tells the first convict, "We don't know what you have done, but we wouldn't have you starved to death for it, poor miserable fellow creature." It is the convict who recognizes the "goodness" of Pip rather than the guiltiness of Pip. He sees in Pip someone who brought him food and kept his secret. This may be the reason why the convict confessed to be the one who stole the pork pie.

Study Questions

1. What is the occasion for having dinner guests at the Gargery's?

2. What makes Pip uncomfortable during the Christmas dinner?

3. Who comes to the door just as Mrs. Joe is inviting the guests to taste her pork pie?

4. Why does Pip think the soldiers have come to his house?

5. Why have the soldiers actually come to the Gargery house?

6. When the two convicts are found, what are they doing?

7. What does the second convict claim the first convict tried to do to him?

8. How does Joe feel toward the first convict?

9. Who takes the blame for stealing the food from Mrs. Joe?

10. Where are the convicts taken?

Answers

1. The occasion is Christmas Day.

2. The dinner guests make references to Pip that he is not grateful for what his sister has done for him. Pip also is fearful about the discovery of the missing food.

3. The sergeant and his solders arrive at the door just as Mrs. Joe goes to get her pork pie.

4. Pip thinks the soldiers have come to arrest him for stealing.

5. The soldiers need some handcuffs repaired and have come to ask the blacksmith to do the job.

6. The two convicts are fighting one another in a ditch.

7. The second convict claims that the first convict tried to murder him.

8. He feels that he should not starve no matter what he has done.

9. The first convict takes the blame for stealing the food.

10. The two convicts are taken back to the Hulks.

Suggested Essay Topics

1. Describe the Christmas dinner from Pip's point of view.

2. How are the attitudes of Pip and Joe toward the first convict similar? How does the convict's behavior warrant some compassion?

3. What themes are beginning to emerge from these chapters?

Chapters 6 and 7

New Characters:

Mr. Wopsle's Great-Aunt: *keeps an evening school in the village and also runs a general store*

Biddy: *runs Mr. Wopsle's great-aunt's general store and is her granddaughter; she is an orphan*

Miss Havisham: *mysterious rich lady who lives in town and leads a secluded life*

Summary

Pip is one year older, and although he attends Mr. Wopsle's great-aunt's evening school in the village, it is Biddy who teaches him to read and write. Joe and Pip sit by the hearth and Pip writes Joe a letter. Joe is impressed by Pip's awkward but scholarly endeavor and praises him. Pip asks Joe to read it, but Joe can only read the letters "JO." Pip realizes that Joe can neither read nor write. Pip asks him about his schooling and Joe relates his past to Pip. He tells that his father was a drunkard and made him go to work instead of attending school. He beat Joe and his mother; they left him many times, but he would always come and get them. Joe began working as a blacksmith at a very young age. His father died, then his mother. Joe tells Pip that after living alone he began to notice Pip's sister trying to raise Pip by herself. The people in the village talked about how she was bringing Pip up "by hand." So Joe began to see Pip's sister, married her, and encouraged her to bring the "poor little child" with her to the forge. Joe, caring for Pip as if he were his son, would readily take Pip's punishments if he could. Pip cries, realizing the amount of love Joe has for him. Joe then asks Pip to teach him to read and write, but it must be done secretly because Mrs. Joe does not want anyone to be a scholar in her household. Pip feels a new admiration for Joe.

Because Uncle Pumblechook is a bachelor, Mrs. Joe helps him do his shopping. Upon returning from one of their shopping trips, Mrs. Joe tells Joe and Pip that when Uncle Pumblechook went to pay his rent to Miss Havisham she asked if he knew of a boy who could come and play. Uncle Pumblechook recommended Pip, and he is to go to her house the next morning. Mrs. Joe scrubs and cleans Pip, reminds him that he should be grateful, and sends him off with Mr. Pumblechook who will take him to Miss Havisham's house the next day.

Analysis

Joe's characterization is further developed when he relates his past to Pip. Joe, much like Pip, has had a difficult childhood. The abuse from his alcoholic father makes Joe have a special tenderness for Pip, and this is probably the reason he married Pip's sister. Joe's education also suffered during his youth resulting in his inability to read and write. The knowledge of Joe's past causes Pip to have a new admiration for him.

Pip states in Chapter 6 that he loves Joe and that he "ought to tell Joe the whole truth. Yet I did not...for fear of losing Joe's confidence." Characterization is further developed when Pip states, "I was too cowardly to do what I knew to be right, as I had been too cowardly to avoid doing what I knew to be wrong."

Pip's life is again out of his control when he learns from Mrs. Joe and Uncle Pumblechook that he is to go to Miss Havisham's to play. Pip has no idea why he is going to her house to play. Dickens intentionally leaves many questions unanswered with each chapter. This technique purposely builds suspense with the foreshadowing of future events, leaves mysterious questions unanswered, and introduces new characters right at the end of a chapter.

Study Questions

1. Why didn't Pip tell Joe the truth concerning the convict and the theft?

2. What is probably the reason that Joe married Pip's sister?

3. What does Mr. Wopsle's great-aunt run in the evenings?

4. Even though Pip attends the evening school, who actually teaches Pip how to read and write?

5. What does Pip find out about Joe's education?

6. What is the only word that Joe can read?

7. Pip agrees to help Joe learn to read and write. Why must they keep it a secret from Mrs. Joe?

8. What news do Uncle Pumblechook and Mrs. Joe bring home to Pip?

9. What does Miss Havisham ask Pip to come there to do?

10. Who first takes Pip to Miss Havisham's house?

Answers

1. Pip did not tell Joe the truth because he was afraid of losing Joe's confidence and friendship.

2. Joe probably married Pip's sister because he felt sympathy for Pip and how he was being treated.

3. Mr. Wopsle's great-aunt runs an evening school.

4. Biddy is the one who teaches Pip how to read and write.

5. Pip, after writing a crude letter to Joe, realizes that Joe cannot read or write.

6. "JO" is the only word that Joe can read.

7. Joe's education must be kept a secret from Mrs. Joe because

she resents anyone being better than she is.

8. The news is that Pip is to go to Miss Havisham's house the next morning.

9. Miss Havisham wants Pip to come there and play.

10. Uncle Pumblechook is the one who first takes Pip to Miss Havisham's house.

Suggested Essay Topics

1. How does Dickens build suspense in his novel?

2. Explain how the bond between Pip and Joe becomes even stronger.

3. Describe Joe's relationship with Pip and his relationship with his wife.

Chapters 8 and 9

New Characters:

Estella: *a young girl about the same age as Pip who lives with Miss Havisham*

Summary

Pip goes home with Mr. Pumblechook and is sent directly to bed. In the morning Pip is given bread crumbs and diluted milk while Mr. Pumblechook drills him in math. At ten o'clock they go to Miss Havisham's house which is dismal and closed up. Some of the windows are walled up while most of the remaining ones are encased in iron bars. The courtyard in front is also barred. There is an old brewery on one side of the house and the unkempt grounds are overgrown with tangled weeds. Pip and Mr. Pumblechook stand at the gate waiting to be let in. Estella lets only Pip in and turns Mr. Pumblechook away. As Pip and Estella walk toward the house, she tells him that it is called Satis, which means "enough" and that "when it was given that whoever had this house could want nothing else." Even though the sun is shinning outside, Estella leads

Pip into the dark house lit only by candles. She knocks on a door and is instructed to enter. Pip is to go in by himself, and Estella leaves.

As he enters the sunless room lighted with wax candles, he sees that it is a woman's dressing room. Sitting at her dressing table is Miss Havisham. She is dressed in a white dress which is now yellow with age. Her hair is white, and a yellowed veil hangs from her hair. Everything that should be white is faded and yellow. The flowers in her hair have withered long ago, and her dress hangs loosely about her body as if her body has also withered away since she put it on. Pip also notices that other dresses are scattered about the room and packing trunks are left open. As he glances around the room, he discovers that all the clocks have stopped at twenty minutes to nine.

Miss Havisham tells him that she needs diversion, and he is to play. Pip, feeling awkward and afraid, does not know what to play. Miss Havisham sends for Estella and makes them play a card game called "Beggar my Neighbour," which is the only game Pip knows. Estella is proud and insulted that she has to play with such a common boy. Even thought they are about the same age, Estella insults Pip by calling him a "common labouring-boy" and makes fun of him.

When Pip is permitted to leave, Miss Havisham tells him to return in six days to play again. Estella takes him downstairs, gives him some food, and leaves him alone while he eats. He has never before thought of himself as coarse or common, and because Pip is a very sensitive boy, Estella has hurt him deeply. He buries his face in his sleeve and cries. After eating, Pip explores the brewery when a strange thing happens to him. He imagines Miss Havisham hanging from a wooden beam by her neck. He runs from the building and is brought back to reality by the sunlight outside and Estella approaching with the keys to let him out of the gate.

Pip walks the four miles home and is met by Mr. Pumblechook and Mrs. Joe who want to know all the details of his visit. Pip knows that they would not understand what really happened, so he makes up a story about Miss Havisham sitting in a black velvet coach, huge dogs eating veal-cutlets out of a silver basket, and playing with flags. When Joe comes into the house from the forge, Pip feels guilty for

lying. Mrs. Joe and Mr. Pumblechook discuss the possibility of Pip getting some money from Miss Havisham if he stays in her favor. Pip confesses to Joe that he had been lying. Joe gives Pip a lecture about lying. It was a memorable day for Pip, and it changed his life forever.

Analysis

Dickens goes into lengthy description of Satis House and Miss Havisham. It is ironic that the name of the house means "enough" and it, as well as Miss Havisham, appear so neglected and in need. She lives in a dark, timeless world. Similes are used to help the reader picture Miss Havisham by stating that "not even the withered bridal dress on the collapsed form could have looked so like grave-clothes, or the long veil so like a shroud. So she sat, corpselike, as we played at cards; the frillings and trimmings on her bridal dress, looking like earthy paper."

Until this day at Miss Havisham's, Pip has been content with Joe and his life at the forge. But, for the first time, he is made to realize that his hands are coarse, and his boots are thick, and that he is just a "common labouring-boy." Estella, proud and cold, has succeeded in making him feel dissatisfied with his position in life for the first time.

Again, the theme of good and evil resurfaces when Pip exaggerates his experiences at Satis House to Mrs. Joe and Uncle Pumblechook. Lying is evil, and he cannot lie to Joe. The gentle, honest, always good Joe cautions that lies do not make a person uncommon, and he should never lie again. The bond between them is strong, and Pip wants Joe to see him as "good."

Study Questions

1. What is the meaning of Satis?
2. At what time have all the clocks in Miss Havisham's house stopped?
3. Who opens the gate to let Pip in at Miss Havisham's?
4. What game does Pip play with Estella?
5. How is Miss Havisham dressed?
6. How does Estella hurt Pip's feelings?
7. Who does Pip imagine he sees hanging from a beam in the brewery?

8. Why does Pip lie to Mrs. Joe and Uncle Pumblechook about his day at Miss Havisham's?

9. Pip cannot lie to whom?

10. On what subject does Joe lecture Pip?

Answers

1. "Satis" in Satis House means enough.

2. All the clocks in Miss Havisham's house have stopped at twenty minutes to nine.

3. Estella opens the gate for Pip.

4. Estella and Pip play a card game called "Beggar my Neighbor."

5. Miss Havisham is dressed in a faded and yellowed wedding dress.

6. Estella calls Pip "boy" and brings attention to his thick boots and coarse hands.

7. Pip imagines he sees Miss Havisham hanging by her neck from a beam in the brewery.

8. He lies because he is afraid of being misunderstood. He also feels that he cannot relate the private lives of Miss Havisham and Estella to Mrs. Joe and Uncle Pumblechook.

9. Pip cannot lie to Joe.

10. Joe gently lectures Pip about honesty and not telling lies.

Suggested Essay Topics

1. How does Pip's day at Miss Havisham's change him forever?

2. Compare Miss Havisham and Satis House.

3. Describe Estella and her effect on Pip.

4. Relate examples of Joe's goodness.

Chapters 10 and 11

New Characters:

Stranger at the Three Jolly Bargemen: *questions Joe about Pip and stirs his rum with Joe's file*

Mrs. Camilla, Cousin Raymond, Sarah Pocket, Georgiana Pocket: *relatives of Miss Havisham who come to visit her on her birthday in hopes that they will be rewarded monetarily one day*

Gentleman coming downstairs at Miss Havisham's: *stops Pip on his way up to see Miss Havisham*

Pale Young Gentleman: *fights with Pip in the garden at Miss Havisham's*

Summary

Following his visit to Miss Havisham's, Pip decides to learn everything he can to become uncommon. Mr. Wopsle's great-aunt's evening school offers him no educational advantages or learning. The great-aunt frequently falls asleep, and the students do as they please. Biddy tries to get the students to read what they can, but all is chaos. Pip asks Biddy if she will teach him everything she knows. Every evening they meet and discuss prices, copy letters, and read.

One Saturday Pip goes to the Three Jolly Bargemen, a public house in the village, in order to walk home with Joe. Joe is seated with Mr. Wopsle and a mysterious stranger. Upon hearing Joe call Pip's name, the stranger is extremely interested in Pip. He looks at no one but Pip. When no one else is looking at him except Pip, he begins to stir his rum and water with Joe's file. Pip is spellbound by the realization that this man knows his convict—the one he helped on the marshes. As Pip and Joe get up to leave the public house, the stranger stops them and gives Pip a shilling wrapped up in some crumpled paper, which turns out to be two one-pound notes.

On Wednesday Pip returns to Miss Havisham's. Estella again opens the gate for him, but takes him to a different room filled with Miss Havisham's relatives. Pip detects a coldness towards him as he waits in the room. Finally, Estella escorts Pip to another room

upstairs. While going up the stairs, Pip and Estella encounter a large man coming down the stairs. They pause, observing one another, and the man admonishes Pip to "behave himself." Pip and Estella proceed up the stairs and into a room with a large table in the center. There, Pip is instructed to aid Miss Havisham in walking around and around the long table. In the center of the table is a decayed bridal cake infested with beetles, spiders, and mice. As they walk, Miss Havisham tells Pip that when she dies, she is going to be laid on that table.

The relatives are ushered in, but Miss Havisham and Pip continue to walk. They attempt a conversation with the ever-moving Miss Havisham, but she cuts their remarks short. The reader learns that the relatives have come because it is Miss Havisham's birthday, and they are all hoping that after her death, they will receive some monetary compensation for their pretended concern over her. It seems that only one relative has never come to inquire about Miss Havisham, and he is Matthew Pocket. Miss Havisham assures everyone that when she is dead that he too will be there, and she points out where each relative will stand around the table. The relatives are dismissed, and Pip is ushered out into the decayed and tangled garden where he encounters a pale young gentleman who challenges him to a fight by butting him in the stomach. The fight is humorous, and with each punch, Pip succeeds in repeatedly knocking the boy down. The young man finally declares the fight over and Pip the winner. Estella escorts Pip to the gate.

Analysis

Because Pip has become dissatisfied with himself and his station in life, he has decided to do something about it by getting Biddy to help him become "uncommon." Pip does not simply accept his station in life but begins to strive to change his destiny which brings a new theme into focus—that of what it takes to make a person a gentleman or a lady. Pip is correctly convinced that the first step to becoming a gentleman is education.

Dickens continually introduces characters by describing them instead of giving them a name. The reader finds out later who the characters are, but by introducing them in this manner, the author is able to maintain suspense and interest within the reader.

In these two chapters, we meet a stranger who stirs his drink with a file, a large gentleman coming down the stairs at Miss Havisham's, and a pale young gentleman who fights with Pip. The novel is written much like a gigantic puzzle that will be put together as the chapters reveal bits and pieces of information. Finally, a name is given to each of these characters, and the entire picture, or novel, comes together.

Pip is affected by all the people he encounters, either negatively or positively. The direction of his life has been changed by his visit to Miss Havisham and by the arrogant and proud Estella. Even though he does not understand, at the time, what effect a new character will have, it is certain that sooner or later, the character will reappear and affect Pip's life.

Study Questions

1. What does the mysterious stranger at the Three Jolly Bargemen stir his drink with?

2. What does the stranger give to Pip?

3. How does Estella treat Pip in these two chapters?

4. What is the Three Jolly Bargemen?

5. Who are the people waiting with Pip in the large room at Miss Havisham's?

6. On what occasion are these people visiting Miss Havisham?

7. Describe what Pip sees on the bridal table.

8. Where does Miss Havisham want to be laid when she is dead?

9. What does Miss Havisham ask Pip to do on this visit?

10. What do Pip and the pale young gentleman do?

Answers

1. The mysterious stranger stirs his drink with Joe's file.

2. The stranger gives Pip a new shilling wrapped in two one-pound notes.

3. Going up the stairs to see Miss Havisham, Estella slaps Pip and calls him a "little coarse monster." As she is escorting him out after his visit, she allows him to kiss her on the cheek.

4. Located in the village, the Three Jolly Bargemen is a public-house with a bar.

5. The people waiting with Pip are relatives by the name of Pocket.

6. They are visiting Miss Havisham because it is her birthday.

7. Pip sees a yellowed and decayed wedding cake infested and overrun with spiders, beetles, and mice.

8. When Miss Havisham dies she wants to be laid on the long reception table where the cake is.

9. Miss Havisham asks Pip to help her walk around and around the bridal table.

10. Pip and the pale young gentleman have a humorous fight with Pip being the victor.

Suggested Essay Topics

1. Explain how Pip's visit to Miss Havisham has affected him.

2. What does Dickens use to create suspense and interest in his novel?

3. Discuss Pip's encounter with Miss Havisham's relatives, and what were his impressions?

4. Explain how humor is used concerning Pip and the pale young gentleman?

Chapters 12 and 13

Summary

Pip worries about the fight with the pale young gentleman and wonders if he will be severely disciplined for hitting the young boy. He is afraid to return to Miss Havisham's, but after searching the scene of the fight and surveying the overlooking windows, Pip decides that no punishment is to come to him. He finds that Miss Havisham must now be pushed in a wheelchair when she becomes too tired to walk, and that sometimes they walk for as long as three hours. Pip returns every other day for about eight to ten months, and as they walk, they talk.

Miss Havisham often asks Pip if Estella is growing prettier. She then whispers to Estella to "break their hearts, my pride and hope, break their hearts and have no mercy!" After noticing one day that he has grown taller, Miss Havisham asks that Joe accompany Pip on his next visit. She believes that he should become apprenticed to the blacksmith as soon as possible.

While at home at the forge, Pip's sister and Uncle Pumblechook discuss what they might gain as a result of Pip's visits with Miss Havisham. The next day Joe, dressed in his Sunday clothes, and Pip go to Miss Havisham's. Mrs. Joe is angry because she was not invited to accompany them and goes to visit Mr. Pumblechook. Pip is embarrassed by the way Joe looks in his clothes and decides that he "looked far better in his working dress." He is again embarrassed when, instead of directly talking to Miss Havisham, he answers her through Pip. Miss Havisham pays Joe 25 guineas for his apprenticeship. Pip asks if he is to come again to Satis House, and Miss Havisham answers, "No."

Pip and Joe leave and go to Uncle Pumblechook's where Joe tries to make Mrs. Joe believe that Miss Havisham sent her compliments to her. He lets Mrs. Joe have the money, and Mr. Pumblechook makes all of them go to the Town Hall to have Pip made a bound apprentice legally. After leaving the Town Hall, Pumblechook takes all the credit for getting the money from Miss Havisham for Pip's apprenticeship and insists that they all have dinner at the Blue Boar. Pip goes to bed that night feeling "truly wretched," and with a strong feeling "that I should never like Joe's trade. I had liked it once, but once was not now."

Analysis

The theme of right and wrong surfaces again as Pip worries about what will be done to him for fighting with the pale young gentleman. He envisions Miss Havisham herself or hired mercenaries coming to punish him for his deed. He remembers his station in life is that of a common laboring boy and that the other boy is a gentleman.

Pip's unhappiness and dissatisfaction become more evident when he is embarrassed by the appearance of Joe at Miss Havisham's and by the fact that Joe would not communicate directly with her. He makes the statement that "I was ashamed of the dear good fellow." Pip would like for Joe to be something he is not. Even though Pip wishes that Joe were more genteel and more knowledgeable, Joe himself is satisfied with his station in life and only is made to feel uncomfortable when trying to be something he is not.

Pumblechook is portrayed as pretentious and wanting credit where none is due.

Joe, trying to soften Mrs. Joe's feelings for not being asked to Miss Havisham's, makes her feel that Mrs. Havisham's health prevented her from including Mrs. Joe in her invitation. He is always considerate of Mrs. Joe no matter how she treats him.

The apprenticeship system was a means of training young men for a trade or occupation. The master, or teacher, would usually be paid a fee, and he would specify the number of years it would take to complete the training. The indenture papers were a binding contract.

Study Questions

1. What does Pip worry about before he returns to Miss Havisham's?

2. What do Miss Havisham and Pip do every visit?

3. Why does Miss Havisham ask Pip to bring Joe to her house?

4. What does apprenticeship mean?

5. What does Miss Havisham pay Joe for Pip's apprenticeship?

6. How does Joe embarrass Pip at Miss Havisham's?

7. Who does Pip confide in?

8. What does Miss Havisham instruct Estella to do?

9. Who takes the credit for Pip's apprenticeship?

10. How does Pip feel about his apprenticeship to Joe?

Answers

1. Pip worries that he will get punished for fighting with the pale young gentleman.

2. Miss Havisham and Pip walk, sometimes as long as three hours.

3. Miss Havisham wants Joe to come to her house because she wants to pay for Pip's apprenticeship.

4. An apprentice is someone who is bound by law to work for a master in order to learn his trade.

5. Miss Havisham pays Joe 25 guineas.

6. Pip is embarrassed because of the way Joe is dressed and because Joe will not talk directly to Miss Havisham.

7. Pip confides in Biddy.

8. Miss Havisham instructs Estella to "break their hearts and have no mercy."

9. Uncle Pumblechook takes the credit for Pip's apprenticeship.

10. Pip is extremely unhappy about his apprenticeship to Joe.

Suggested Essay Topics

1. How has Pip changed? Give examples of his dissatisfaction concerning his life and his family.

2. Explain what being an apprentice means and how this affects Pip.

3. Write a character analysis of Uncle Pumblechook.

4. Describe the relationship between Joe and Mrs. Joe.

Chapters 14 and 15

New Characters:

Dolge Orlick: *a journeyman working for Joe who has great strength and is always slouching; he is 25 years of age and dislikes Pip*

Summary

Pip begins his apprenticeship to Joe and feels that "it is a most miserable thing to feel ashamed of home." Pip realizes that he could have run off and become a sailor, but it is because of Joe that he does not. He fears that Estella will come to the forge and see him at his dirtiest, and he imagines her face in the flames of the fire in the forge. Pip is still trying to learn all he can to become uncommon, receiving lessons from not only Biddy, but Mr. Wopsle as well. Everything Pip learns he tries to teach to Joe because he "wanted to make Joe less ignorant and common, that he might be worthier of my society and less open to Estella's reproach."

Every Sunday Pip and Joe go out to the marshes, and Pip tries to teach Joe. Although Joe never retains much knowledge, he always enjoys this time with Pip. One afternoon Pip suggests that he ought to return to Miss Havisham's to thank her for all she has done for him. Joe does not think he should return for fear that she might think he wants something from her. He finally agrees to allow a half day holiday so that Pip might go.

Orlick, a large, slouching journeyman, overhears Joe give Pip permission to leave early and accuses Joe of favoritism. Joe agrees to allow Orlick off for half a day also. When Mrs. Joe hears Joe's decision, she begins to shout at Joe and Orlick. Orlick responds by calling her "a foul shrew," causing Mrs. Joe to go into a "rampage." Joe tries to get Orlick to "let her alone," but they continue to shriek at one another. Mrs. Joe demands to know why Joe is not taking up for her. Joe has no choice now but to fight Orlick. Joe knocks him to the ground and then carries Mrs. Joe, who has fainted, into the house.

Pip goes into town looking forward to seeing Estella, which is the real reason he wants to go see Miss Havisham. But it is Miss Sarah Pocket who comes to the gate instead of Estella. Pip is escorted in to see Miss Havisham where she says, "I hope you want nothing? You'll get nothing." Pip assures her that he does not, and he only wants to thank her for his apprenticeship. She invites him to return to see her on his birthday. She notices Pip looking for Estella and tells him that she is abroad becoming a lady.

On his way home, Pip runs into Mr. Wopsle, and they both go to Mr. Pumblechook's to discuss a book that Mr. Wopsle has just purchased. About eleven at night, Mr. Wopsle and Pip start home from the village. The night is shrouded with a heavy mist, very wet and thick. They meet Orlick, also heading for home, and the three of them walk together. Cannon fire is heard in the distance as another escaped convict is announced. Hearing a commotion at the

Three Jolly Bargemen, Mr. Wopsle goes in to inquire, runs out, and announces that something has happened at Pip's house. They run home to find the house filled with people and Mrs. Joe lying on the floor in front of the fireplace unconscious. She has been struck on the back of the head with a tremendous blow.

Analysis

Pip's reasons for educating Joe are not for Joe but for himself. Pip's values are changing, and honesty and goodness are not enough. Pip is trying to change himself, and he feels that in order to become uncommon, he must also change those around him. He assumes that Joe, too, wants to be different. Pip, who at one time was very sensitive to Joe and others, is now very self-centered. It is interesting to note that Joe never complains of their Sunday lessons but seems to view them simply as an opportunity to enjoy Pip's company.

A sinister character is introduced in these chapters. Orlick not only does not like Pip, but argues with Mrs. Joe and even fights with Joe. The result of the confrontation reveals Joe's fairness and goodness as he agrees to allow Orlick to take off half a day, and he defends Mrs. Joe against Orlick's remarks. Up until these chapters, Joe has been portrayed as almost childlike—simple and trusting. Now the reader sees him pressured into fighting which only adds to his character and is not a negative quality in him.

The attack on Mrs. Joe at the end of Chapter 15 leaves the reader with anticipation and questions. Could the firing of the cannons on the Hulks be foreshadowing or is Dickens presenting several possibilities concerning the identity of the attacker?

Study Questions

1. Why does Pip want to educate Joe?

2. What is the reason Pip gives Joe for wanting to return to Miss Havisham's?

3. What is the real reason he wants to return to Miss Havisham's?

4. Who meets Pip at Miss Havisham's gate?

5. Where is Estella?

6. When does Miss Havisham invite Pip to return?

7. What is the name of Joe's journeyman at the forge?

8. Who causes the fight between Orlick and Joe?

9. Who joins Pip and Mr. Wopsle on their walk home?

10. What happens at home while Pip is in the village?

Answers

1. Pip wants to educate Joe to make him less ignorant and common. Pip is also afraid of what Estella would think of Joe.

2. Pip tells Joe that he wants to thank Miss Havisham for his apprenticeship.

3. Pip really wants to see Estella again.

4. Miss Sarah Pocket meets Pip at Miss Havisham's gate.

5. Estella has been sent abroad to become a lady.

6. Miss Havisham tells Pip that he may return on his birthday.

7. Joe's journeyman's name is Orlick.

8. Mrs. Joe causes the fight between Orlick and Joe. She demands that Joe defend her honor.

9. Orlick joins Pip and Mr. Wopsle on their walk home.

10. Mrs. Joe is struck on the head and left unconscious on the floor.

Suggested Essay Topics

1. Write a character sketch of Orlick.

2. Describe Pip's return visit to see Miss Havisham.

3. Describe Joe and Pip's relationship.

Chapters 16 and 17

Summary

After Mrs. Joe is attacked, Pip feels guilt and goes over and over

the evidence and circumstances of the attack. Joe had been at the Three Jolly Bargemen; Orlick had been in town and even walked home with him and Mr. Wopsle. Nothing had been taken or disturbed at the house; however, an important piece of evidence was found beside Mrs. Joe—a convict's leg iron. After looking at the iron, Joe decides that it had been filed off a long time ago. Pip believes that the iron belongs to the first convict, but he does not believe that his convict is the one who attacked his sister. Pip suspects the attacker to be either Orlick or the stranger who stirred his rum with Joe's file, and he feels guilty because he had provided the weapon.

Mrs. Joe is ill for many months with multiple complications. Her sight, hearing, and memory are impaired, and her speech is unintelligible. Because Mrs. Joe has to have constant care, Biddy moves into the house to take care of her and the household. During this time, Mrs. Joe keeps tracing on her slate a figure that looks like a "T." Pip finally determines that it could represent a hammer. Mrs. Joe does not want a hammer, but she wants to see Orlick every time she draws the figure. When Orlick comes into the house, she does not appear angry or disturbed, but seems humble and almost kind to him.

Time passes and it is Pip's birthday. He returns to see Miss Havisham, who gives him a guinea. Estella is still abroad. Pip becomes accustomed to his life at the forge and almost begins to accept it. He begins to notice that Biddy, though common, has changed and become pretty. He invites her to take a walk on the marshes on Sunday, and it is on this walk that he confides to her his desire to be a gentleman. She listens patiently, but asks Pip if he should not be happy as he is.

Pip then relates to her that the reason he wants to become a gentleman is because of his admiration of Estella. He promises always to tell Biddy everything, but Biddy replies, "Till you're a gentleman." They begin to walk home and come upon Orlick. He offers to walk home with them, but Biddy tells him that she would rather he not accompany them. Biddy is afraid that Orlick is attracted to her, and he frightens her. Pip declines his offer, and they walk home with Orlick following at a distance. About the time Pip begins to consider keeping company with Biddy, becoming partners with Joe, and settling down to a happy, contented life at the forge, his thoughts return to Miss Havisham and Estella. Pip still hopes that maybe Miss Havisham will help him become a gentleman after his apprenticeship is over.

Analysis

After Biddy moves into the forge, Pip begins to notice her. She has become pretty in an honest, sincere way. Biddy is wise for her years, and after hearing Pip's desire to be a gentleman replies, "But don't you think you are happier as you are?" She tells Pip that having to change for someone is an indication that the person is not worth it.

Pip notices how different Biddy is from Estella. Biddy is always the same, never temperamental or changing, and he realizes that if it were not for Estella, he would probably consider keeping company with her.

Study Questions

1. What important piece of evidence was left beside Mrs. Joe's body?

2. Mrs. Joe lives, but how is she afflicted?

3. What does Mrs. Joe repeatedly draw on her slate?

4. When Mrs. Joe draws this figure, who does she want to see?

5. What does the "T" represent?

6. Who are the two people Pip suspects could be Mrs. Joe's attacker?

7. Who comes to live at the forge and cares for Mrs. Joe?

8. When Pip returns to see Miss Havisham on his birthday, what does she give him?

9. Who does Pip confide in that he wants to be a gentleman?

10. What is the reason that Pip wants to be a gentleman?

Answers

1. A convict's filed off leg-iron was found next to her body.

2. Her sight, hearing, memory, and speech are impaired.

3. Mrs. Joe repeatedly draws a figure that looks like a "T."

4. When Mrs. Joe draws a "T," she wants to see Orlick.

5. The "T" represents a hammer.

6. Pip suspects Orlick or the stranger who stirred his rum with a file at the Three Jolly Bargeman.

7. Biddy comes to live at the forge and cares for Mrs. Joe.

8. Miss Havisham gives Pip a guinea on his birthday.

9. Pip confides to Biddy that he wants to be a gentleman.

10. Estella is the reason Pip wants to be a gentleman.

Suggested Essay Topics

1. Explain the relationship between Pip and Biddy.

2. Discuss the attack on Mrs. Joe and how it affected Pip.

3. Write a character sketch of Biddy.

Chapters 18 and 19

New Characters:

Mr. Jaggers: *a lawyer from London who informs Pip of his great expectations; he is to be Pip's guardian*

Mr. Trabb: *a tailor in the village who makes Pip's new clothes*

Mr. Trabb's Boy: *a young boy who works for Mr. Trabb and treats Pip with disdain*

Summary

Pip has been an apprentice to Joe for four years. He, Joe, Mr. Wopsle, and some other villagers are in the Three Jolly Bargemen enjoying Mr. Wopsle's dramatic reading about a murder case in the newspaper. A stranger challenges the group concerning jumping to conclusions about a person's guilt and makes Mr. Wopsle feel insignificant. The stranger asks for Joe and Pip to accompany him outside where he tells them that he has some news for Pip. They return to the forge and sit at the kitchen table where he offers money to end Pip's apprenticeship. Joe refuses the money.

Pip recognizes the stranger as the gentleman who was coming downstairs at Miss Havisham's on Pip's second visit. The stranger reveals his name as that of Mr. Jaggers, a lawyer from London. He then informs Pip that Pip has acquired great expectations and will leave for London in one week. He tells Pip that Jaggers is to be his guardian, and he gives Pip 20 guineas in order that he might go into the village and have new clothes made. His tutor in London will be Mr. Matthew Pocket. Pip recognizes the name as belonging to the cousin of Miss Havisham.

Mr. Jaggers tells Pip that there are three stipulations to the great fortune. One, he must always keep the name of Pip; two, the name of the benefactor will remain a secret until that person decides to reveal it to him; and three, Pip is never to inquire or question anyone concerning the identity of the benefactor. Pip agrees to the stipulations, and Mr. Jaggers again offers some money to Joe who becomes angry that Mr. Jaggers would even think that Joe would take money for Pip's good fortune.

Pip is certain that it must be Miss Havisham who is the benefactor, but he says nothing. After breakfast the next morning, Joe and Pip throw his indenture papers into the fire. The next few days are spent getting ready to travel to London. He goes to Mr. Trabb's tailor shop in order to purchase new clothes. After learning that Pip has money, the tailor treats him quite politely. The tailor begins to call Pip "Sir," and Pip decides that money has great power.

Pip goes to see Mr. Pumblechook, who has already heard of his good fortune. Mr. Pumblechook fawns over him by calling him "My dear friend," and shaking his hand often. Pip goes to see Miss Havisham to tell her that he will be leaving. Sarah Pocket hovers about them as they talk, and Miss Havisham seems to relish the idea of making Mrs. Pocket think she is giving money to Pip. At the end of the week Pip is off to London feeling sorry for his ingratitude toward Joe, but looking forward to his great expectations.

Analysis

The novel is divided into three distinct phases or stages in Pip's life. The first stage ends here with Chapter 19. These first chapters represent innocence of childhood in Pip. The spiritual values given

to him in his childhood in the first stage of Pip's life will now be replaced with the material values of the wealthy. However, Pip is already guilty of false pride and self-deception by the time he leaves for London. Pip feels both guilt and elation—elation that he is given the chance to become a gentleman and guilt for not being happy at the forge with Joe.

Another possible theme emerges at the close of the first stage of Pip's life—the theme of money and its affects on the possessor and those who are acquainted with the possessor. People treat people of wealth differently, as Pip discovers with both Mr. Trabb the tailor and Mr. Pumblechook.

Pip has his only argument with Biddy when he asks her to help improve Joe. Pip has acquired an air of superiority, and he wants to share his great expectations by moving Joe up in society. However, he is disregarding Joe's pride and his happiness with his station in life. When Biddy argues against improving Joe, Pip accuses Biddy of envy. Pip refuses to see her wisdom. Biddy knows that money and social standing do not guarantee goodness or happiness. Pip, on the other hand, is experiencing inner conflict. He is dissatisfied with his life at the forge, but he recognizes the goodness in Joe and Biddy and feels guilt for wanting to leave them.

There are many circumstances that point to Miss Havisham as Pip's "fairy godmother." Miss Havisham's lawyer is Mr. Jaggers. When Pip comes to see her, she already knows the conditions of the inheritance. She is the only rich person Pip knows, and during Pip's latest visit, she encourages Pip to believe it was she who is the benefactor. Also, his tutor in London is to be Matthew Pocket, a cousin of Miss Havisham.

Study Questions

1. Who informs Pip that he has great expectations?
2. What are the three stipulations of the inheritance?
3. Who is to be Pip's guardian while he is in London?
4. Who is to be Pip's tutor while he is in London?
5. When Mr. Jaggers offers Joe money to compensate for the loss of Pip's services, what does the blacksmith do?

6. Who does Pip believe is his benefactor?

7. Why does Pip visit Mr. Trabb, the tailor?

8. How does the reader know that Biddy understands Joe better than Pip does?

9. How has the behavior of Mr. Pumblechook and Mr. Trabb changed toward Pip?

10. Where is Pip going at the end of Chapter 19?

Answers

1. Mr. Jaggers, a lawyer from London, informs Pip of his great expectations.

2. The three conditions of the inheritance are as follows:

   He must always keep the name of Pip.

   The name of the benefactor will remain a secret until that person decides to reveal it to him.

   Pip is never to inquire or question anyone concerning the identity of the benefactor.

3. Mr. Jaggers is to be Pip's guardian.

4. Matthew Pocket is to be Pip's tutor in London.

5. Joe refuses the money and replies that money cannot compensate "for the loss of the little child."

6. Pip believes Miss Havisham to be his benefactor.

7. Pip asks Mr. Trabb to make him new clothes for his journey to London.

8. Pip is forgetting about Joe's pride. Biddy understands Joe's worth as he is.

9. Both men now call him "Sir." They offer the best they have and treat him with new respect—a respect brought about by money.

10. Pip is on his way to London to become more educated and to become a gentleman.

Suggested Essay Topics

1. Explain the circumstances or coincidences that help make Pip believe Miss Havisham is his benefactor.

2. Discuss the first stage of Pip's life. How can this stage be called one of innocence or childhood?

3. Discuss the two settings in the novel—that of Satis House and that of the forge with its marshes. What characters are associated with each, and how do they affect Pip?

Great Expectations Part II

Chapters 20 and 21

New Characters:

Mr. John Wemmick: *Mr. Jagger's clerk in London*

Mr. Pocket, Jr.: *Herbert Pocket, also known as the "pale young gentleman" in Chapters 10 and 11; he is to be Pip's roommate in London*

Summary

Pip, anticipating great expectations, is dismayed with London which is located about five hours from his village. He is not prepared for the ugliness and filthiness of the city. He is brought down a "gloomy" street to Mr. Jaggers' office, described by Pip as "a most dismal place."

Pip tires of waiting for Mr. Jaggers' return and goes walking, where he encounters the jail, Newgate Prison, the gallows, and many people speaking admirably of Mr. Jaggers' ability as a lawyer. After overhearing one remark, "Jaggers would do it if it was to be done," Pip's estimation of his new guardian grows. Pip sees Mr. Jaggers approaching and they walk back together to his office. As they walk through the crowds, Mr. Jaggers admonishes some to stay away, some to tell him nothing more than he wants to hear, and still others that everything is taken care of. He exhibits no sentimentality and detaches himself emotionally from humanity.

Pip is instructed to go to Barnard's Inn and stay with Matthew Pocket's son. In the meantime, he is given cards of tradesmen and told to get any clothes or anything else he might need. Mr. Wemmick walks him to his new living quarters where Pip is disappointed by the run-down, shabby appearance of Barnard's Inn. He was expecting something much finer and grander. Mr. Pocket, Jr., has gone out and Wemmick leaves Pip to wait for his return. Mr. Pocket returns and Pip recognizes him as the "pale young gentleman" he fought with in Miss Havisham's garden.

Analysis

A new setting is presented to the reader and to Pip. Pip is disappointed that the city appears "rather ugly, crooked, narrow, and dirty." He is also dismayed to find that Barnard's Inn, his new lodging place, is also dismal, dilapidated, and run down. His disappointment is tempered when he meets his new roommate and discovers that Herbert Pocket is the "pale young gentleman" who was at Miss Havisham's. Because Herbert is Miss Havisham's relative, Pip is even more certain that she is his benefactor. He feels that he is being made a gentleman so that he will be worthy of Estella. Herbert is friendly and makes Pip feel quite at home.

Pip is impressed with his guardian's popularity among the people and finds that he is a criminal lawyer of great renown. Mr. Jaggers, Pip's guardian, is a dominant force in Pip's new life. To Pip, he is a man of much expertise and power.

Study Questions

1. What is the name of Mr. Jaggers' clerk?
2. What is the name of the "pale young gentleman"?
3. What is Pip's impression of London?
4. What is the name of the inn where Pip is to live?
5. What does Mr. Jaggers give to Pip?
6. Who walks Pip to Barnard's Inn?
7. What kind of lawyer is Mr. Jaggers?

8. Where have Pip and Herbert Pocket met before now?

9. What is Pip's impression of Mr. Jaggers?

10. What is the name of the prison located near Mr. Jaggers' office?

Answers

1. Mr. Wemmick is the name of Mr. Jaggers' clerk.

2. Herbert Pocket is the name of the "pale young gentleman."

3. Pip is disappointed in London. It appears to be crowded, dirty, and dismal.

4. Pip is to stay at Barnard's Inn.

5. Mr. Jaggers gives Pip an allowance and cards of tradesmen with whom he is to deal with for clothes and other things that he should be in need of.

6. Mr. Wemmick walks Pip to Barnard's Inn.

7. Mr. Jaggers is a powerful criminal lawyer.

8. Pip and Herbert Pocket have met in Miss Havisham's garden. They engaged in a humorous fight.

9. Pip realizes, by comments overheard on the street and by observing how Mr. Jaggers treats people, that he is a powerful lawyer. He has a great deal of influence.

10. The prison located near Mr. Jaggers' office is called Newgate Prison.

Suggested Essay Topics

1. Discuss Pip's impressions of London and give examples.

2. Describe Mr. Jaggers' office and how it is representative of the lawyer.

Chapters 22 and 23

New Characters:

Handel: *a name given to Pip by Herbert Pocket*

Belinda Pocket: *wife of Matthew Pocket, quite helpless and dependent upon her nurses; she is obsessed with titles, positions, and luxury*

Matthew Pocket: *Pip's tutor and father of Herbert Pocket*

Flopson and Millers: *two nurses working for Mr. and Mrs. Pocket*

Bentley Drummle: *a student of Mr. Pocket*

Startop: *a student of Mr. Pocket*

Mrs. Coiler: *a "toady" neighbor to Mr. and Mrs. Pocket, also a widow*

Jane: *one of the Pocket's young daughters who helps take care of the other children*

Joe and Fanny: *children of the Pockets*

Sophia: *a servant to Mr. and Mrs. Pocket*

Summary

Herbert and Pip renew their friendship and talk of their fight at Miss Havisham's. Herbert tells Pip that he (Herbert) had been asked to come to Miss Havisham's in order to see if Estella could "take a fancy" to him, but she did not. Pip asks how he felt about the rejection and Herbert replies, "She's (Estella) a Tartar... That girl's hard and haughty and capricious to the last degree, and has been brought up by Miss Havisham to wreak revenge on all the male sex." Herbert tells Pip that Estella is adopted and then tells him Miss Havisham's story.

It seems that Miss Havisham had a half brother who was "riotous, extravagant, undutiful—altogether bad." On his deathbed her father decided to leave the brother a portion of his vast wealth, but the majority went to Miss Havisham. Her half brother wasted his inheritance and held a grudge against Miss Havisham. Then, along came a suitor for Miss Havisham with whom she fell madly in love. His pretenses of being a gentleman were not lost on Matthew Pocket and he warned her of him, after which Miss Havisham ordered him from the house. Meanwhile, the suitor got large sums of money from her and "induced her to buy her brother out of a share in the brewery...at an immense price." The wedding day was set and the preparations made, but the bridegroom did not appear. That was 25 years ago at twenty minutes till nine o'clock, and Miss Havisham has never seen the sun since. It was found later that her suitor and her half brother were in a conspiracy and shared all the money gotten from her.

Pip asks Herbert to help him become a gentleman by offering advice concerning his manners. The first advice that Herbert offers is not to put the knife into your mouth, and a spoon is to be held overhand not under. The advice is offered in such a kind, friendly way that both young men laugh. Herbert decides that a better name for Pip would be Handel because of a piece of music called "The Harmonious Blacksmith" written by Handel.

Herbert takes Pip to Hammersmith where he is to be tutored by Herbert's father. Upon arriving, Pip notices that the household is run completely by the nurses and servants and that Belinda Pocket spends her time reading about titles and peerage. She appears quite helpless and allows the nurses to have complete charge of her seven children, as well as of the household. Mr. Pocket also does not seem to have much authority concerning his family. At supper, Pip meets two other students, Bentley Drummle and Startop.

Analysis

Pip and Herbert get along beautifully. Herbert is both pleasant and friendly. While Pip has a liberal allowance and credit, Herbert is working at a counting-house and earns nothing. He is there looking for possible ways to earn money. Herbert, unlike Pip, seems content with his life, his meager surroundings, and his shabby living place. Herbert is considered a gentleman, yet has little as far as material possessions. Pip's money will provide any of the luxuries that the two will enjoy at Barnard's Inn.

Herbert's mother Belinda has the possessions, but lacks the name and heritage. She is portrayed as "ornamental" and incapable of caring for her children or her household. The reader may begin to wonder if Pip is being developed as something ornamental without much use, for he is not being taught any trade or business as he becomes a gentleman.

During these chapters, the mystery of Miss Havisham and her peculiar behavior is cleared up by Herbert as he relates her story to Pip. The background of Estella still remains a mystery.

Study Questions

1. How does Herbert feel about Estella?
2. What name does Herbert give to Pip?
3. Why is Pip named Handel?
4. What is one of the first lessons Herbert teaches Pip?
5. What relation is Estella to Miss Havisham?
6. Does Miss Havisham have any brothers or sisters?
7. Who did Mr. Havisham leave his vast fortune to after his death?
8. What two men conspired to swindle Miss Havisham out of her money?
9. Which character is obsessed with peerage, titles, and nobility?
10. Who are the other two students living at Matthew Pocket's home?

Answers

1. Herbert thinks she is a "Tartar," trained to break the hearts of young men.
2. Herbert gives Pip the name of Handel.
3. Pip is named Handel after a piece of music called "The Harmonious Blacksmith" written by Handel.
4. Herbert instructs Pip on his table manners—not putting his knife into his mouth and using his spoon underhanded.
5. Estella is adopted and therefore no direct relation to Miss Havisham.
6. Miss Havisham only has a half brother.

7.   Mr. Havisham left the majority of his wealth to Miss Havisham, but he also left some to his son, Miss Havisham's half brother.

8.   Miss Havisham's half brother and her fiancee conspired to swindle her out of her money.

9.   Mrs. Belinda Pocket is obsessed with peerage, titles, and nobility.

10. Startop and Bentley Drummle are the other students at Mr. Pocket's home.

Suggested Essay Topics

1.   What does Pip find out about Miss Havisham's past? Relate her story and its effects upon her life.

2.   Discuss how Herbert's new name for Pip is appropriate.

3.   What is Pip's impression of Belinda and Matthew Pocket's home life.

4.   Compare Belinda Pocket's obsession with social status and nobility with that of Pip's quest for social status and becoming a gentleman.

Chapters 24 and 25

New Character:

Aged Parent: *Mr. Wemmick's deaf father who lives with him at Walworth*

Summary

Pip learns from Mr. Pocket that he is not being trained for any particular profession, but he is to be educated enough to "hold my (Pip) own with the average of young men in prosperous circumstances." Pip decides to keep his room at Barnard's Inn as well as his room at Mr. Pocket's home. He asks Mr. Jaggers for enough money to buy the furniture, which is at the time only rented, at

Barnard's Inn. Mr. Jaggers forces Pip to set the amount and has Mr. Wemmick give him that exact amount.

Wemmick introduces Pip to the other clerks in the office who he finds repulsive and dirty. Wemmick leads Pip back to Mr. Jaggers' office, and they discuss two horrible casts or masks hanging on the wall. Pip learns that the casts had been made after the subjects

had been hanged. Wemmick invites Pip to visit him at his home in Walworth and inquires if Mr. Jaggers has asked him to dinner yet. Wemmick tells Pip that when he does go to dinner at Mr. Jaggers, pay close attention to his housekeeper and "you'll see a wild beast tamed."

Mr. Wemmick takes Pip into court to see Mr. Jaggers at work. Pip feels that Mr. Jaggers bullies not only his clients, but everyone else as well. "The magistrates shivered under a single bite of his finger. Thieves and thieftakers hung in dread rapture on his words, and shrank when a hair of his eyebrows turned in their direction."

In Chapter 25, Dickens describes Bentley Drummle as a "sulky" fellow who is "heavy in figure, movement, and comprehension." Pip finds that Drummle is "idle, proud...and suspicious." On the other hand, Startop is a more delicate young man, and he and Pip get along quite well. As Pip lives and studies with Mr. Pocket, other relatives visit at various times. They all regard Pip with hatred and suspicion.

Pip decides to accept Mr. Wemmick's offer for dinner and a visit. He and Mr. Wemmick walk to Walworth, and Wemmick begins to loosen up and become a totally different if extremely eccentric man. He is exceedingly proud of his small house, called "the Castle." Pip and Wemmick cross over a bridge, and Pip meets the Aged Parent, Mr. Wemmick's father. The Aged Parent is well cared for and is very pleasant. Because the Aged Parent is almost totally deaf, Pip is instructed to keep nodding to him, as this makes him happy. At nine o'clock, they shoot off a cannon called "the Stinger."

When Pip mentions Mr. Jaggers, Wemmick explains that Mr. Jaggers knows nothing of his private life. Wemmick replies, "No: the office is one thing, and private life is another. When I go into the office, I leave the castle behind me, and when I come into the castle, I leave the office behind me."

Analysis

Bentley Drummle is described as a suspicious character and not one that Pip enjoys being around. Pip has now made two new friends—Herbert and Startop. Pip takes up the sport of rowing, a sport that will be used later in the novel.

One character, Mr. Wemmick, is described in these chapters

as having two lives and two personalities. His work with Mr. Jaggers requires him to be a hard, serious man, while his home life offers personal pride and pleasures. He takes great pride in his castle, a small replica of a Gothic castle, which in reality is quite small and insignificant. He is presented as good humored and very caring for his father. Pip learns that Mr. Wemmick enjoys gardening, and the dinner he serves consists of items from his own garden.

Humor is again pictured with the Aged Parent. His inability to hear, Pip's continuous nodding to him, and the enjoyment he gets from the firing of a cannon all create a light hearted tone to the novel.

Study Questions

1. When Pip is invited to Mr. Jaggers' home, who does Wemmick want Pip to notice?
2. Where does Mr. Wemmick live?
3. What does Mr. Wemmick call his home?
4. What does Mr. Wemmick call his father?
5. What does Mr. Wemmick do every night at nine o'clock?
6. What is wrong with Mr. Wemmick's father?
7. What does Mr. Wemmick call his cannon?
8. How is Pip instructed to acknowledge the Aged Parent?
9. Who is the delicate young man being tutored by Mr. Pocket?
10. Who is the sulky young man being tutored by Mr. Pocket?

Answers

1. Wemmick tells Pip to pay particular attention to Mr. Jaggers' housekeeper.
2. Mr. Wemmick lives at Walworth.
3. Mr. Wemmick calls his home "the Castle."
4. Mr. Wemmick calls his father Aged Parent.
5. Mr. Wemmick fires a cannon every night at nine.

6.   Mr. Wemmick's father is almost totally deaf.

7.   Mr. Wemmick calls his cannon the Stinger.

8.   Pip is instructed to keep nodding to the Aged Parent.

9.   Startop is the delicate young man being tutored by Mr. Pocket.

10.   Bentley Drummle is the sulky young man who is tutored by Mr. Pocket.

Suggested Essay Topics

1.   Discuss the dual personalities of Mr. John Wemmick.

2.   Describe Mr. Wemmick's life at Walworth.

3.   Discuss the irony of Mr. Wemmick's labors at the Castle being an acceptable source of pride, and Joe's labors as a blacksmith being unacceptable to Pip.

Chapters 26 and 27

New Characters:

The Spider: *the name Mr. Jaggers gives to Bentley Drummle*

Molly: *Mr. Jaggers' housekeeper who has great strength in her wrists*

Pepper: *also called the Avenger; a servant who works for Pip*

Summary

    Mr. Jaggers invites Pip and his friends to dinner. Pip finds his house bare and neglected. Dinner is served by Mr. Jaggers from a dumbwaiter. Mr. Jaggers takes a liking to Bentley Drummle and refers to the "blotchy, sprawly, sulky fellow" as "the Spider." The housekeeper appears, and Mr. Jaggers tells her to show her wrists to the guests. Her wrists are "disfigured—deeply scarred and scarred across and across." Mr. Jaggers points out that few men or women have the strength that Molly has in her wrists.

    During the course of the dinner, Drummle implies that Pip and Herbert are too free with their money. They reply that they observed

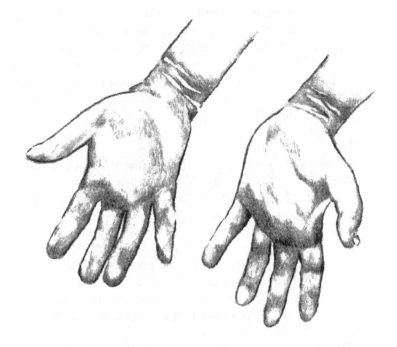

Drummle borrowing money from Startop. Drummle replies that he did, but would never lend money to anyone. The discussion becomes an argument and results in Startop's walking home on one side of the street and Drummle on the other side. As Pip prepares to leave, Mr. Jaggers cautions him by saying, "Don't have too much to do with him (Drummle). Keep as clear of him as you can."

Upon Pip's arrival at Barnard's Inn, he receives a letter from Biddy saying that Joe will be arriving in London the next day. Pip's reception of the letter was "not with pleasure, though I (Pip) was bound to him by so many ties; no; with considerable disturbance, some mortification, and a keen sense of incongruity. If I could have kept him away by paying money, I certainly would have paid money."

Joe arrives the next day feeling awkward around Pip because Pip makes him feel inferior. The dinner is awkward because of Joe's eating habits, and because his hat keeps falling off the mantle causing Joe to grab for it. Joe calls Pip "Sir" and brings news of Mr.

Wopsle and Estella. It seems that Mr. Wopsle has left the church and has gone into "play-acting." Estella has come home and would be glad to see Pip. This news excites Pip so much that he attempts to be a little kinder to Joe, but Joe is ready to leave. Joe leaves after telling Pip that he would not come to London again to see him, but he hoped that Pip would come to see him at the forge where he is more comfortable.

Analysis

There is a sharp contrast between the two dinners Pip attends. Mr. Wemmick completely separates work from home and offers Pip a relaxed and friendly atmosphere with a dinner of home grown foods. On the other hand, Mr. Jaggers' home seems to be an extension of his work. He rules his house, serving dinner himself with the help of only one person. His house is stark with little to offer in the form of pleasure or relaxation. He asks his guests to leave at precisely 9:30 in order for him to study cases. Mr. Jaggers has an obsession about washing his hands with a scented soap after each client or court case. It is almost as if he is washing away any personal involvement that might occur.

The character of Drummle is extended when the young men discuss money and borrowing. Although Jaggers takes a special interest in Drummle, he warns Pip to stay away from him. Mr. Jaggers obviously sees something in Drummle that is fearful. Possibly the fact that Mr. Jaggers deals with criminal clientele so much that it allows him to see something very powerful and sinister in Drummle, something that the reader cannot see.

The visit with Joe illustrates how far Pip has come in his journey from child to gentleman. Pip does not want to see Joe with his "simple dignity" and is very conscious of who might see them together. Pip especially does not want Drummle to see Joe. "So throughout life our worst weaknesses and meannesses are usually committed for the sake of the people whom we most despise." Pip has become a snob and does not, at this point, recognize that Joe is probably more a gentleman than Pip is with his fine clothes, his serving boy, and his extravagant surroundings. It is Joe who recognizes the fact that he does not belong in this atmosphere and invites Pip to come visit him in his environment. It is certain that Joe would never make Pip feel as uncomfortable as Pip is making Joe feel in London. Even Pip realizes that most of the uncomfortableness in Joe is because of him. "...if I had been easier with Joe, Joe would have been easier with me."

Dickens continually adds a little humor to awkward situations. While trying to locate Pip's door, Joe is pictured "breathing in at the keyhole." The episode of Joe's hat, with Joe holding it like a "bird's-nest with eggs in it," also helps relieve the tension that Pip has established within the scene. More humor is added when the hat continually falls from the mantle, and Joe has to grab for it before it hits the floor. The absurdity of the situation brings humor to the reader and mortification for Pip.

Study Questions

1. What name does Mr. Jaggers give Bentley Drummle?
2. Who is Molly?
3. What is unusual about Molly?
4. Who writes Pip a letter?
5. Who is coming to see Pip in London?
6. What keeps falling off the mantle during Pip and Joe's visit?
7. What news does Joe bring Pip?
8. Mr. Jaggers warns Pip not to have much to do with one of his roommates. Who is it?
9. Is Pip glad to see Joe in London?
10. Who travels with Joe to London?

Answers

1. Mr. Jaggers calls Bentley Drummle "the Spider."
2. Molly is Mr. Jaggers' housekeeper.
3. Molly has unusual strength in her wrists.
4. It is Biddy who writes Pip a letter.
5. Joe will be coming to London to visit with Pip.

6. Joe's hat keeps falling off the mantle.

7. Mr. Wopsle has left the church and become an actor, and Estella is home and would like to see him.

8. Mr. Jaggers warns Pip of Bentley Drummle.

9. Pip is embarrassed by Joe's visit and would have done almost anything to keep him from coming.

10. Mr. Wopsle travels with Joe to London.

Suggested Essay Questions

1. Compare and contrast Pip's dinner engagement at the home of Mr. Jaggers with that of Mr. Wemmick.

2. Discuss Joe's visit with Pip. How has Pip changed?

3. What characteristics make a gentleman?

Chapters 28 and 29

Summary

Pip prepares to return immediately to see Estella. He knows he needs to stay at the forge with Joe while he is there, but he invents all kinds of reasons why it would be better for him to stay at the Blue Boar in the village. "I should be an inconvenience at Joe's; I was not expected, and my bed would not be ready; I should be too far from Miss Havisham's, and she was exacting and mightn't like it."

Pip boards the coach heading for home with two convicts who are accompanied by a jailor returning them to the Hulks. Pip recognizes one of the convicts as the mysterious stranger who stirred his rum with Joe's file so long ago at the Three Jolly Bargemen. Pip is relieved that he has changed so much that the convict does not recognize him. As they travel, Pip overhears the two convicts discuss an incident that directly involved Pip. The mysterious convict confesses to the other that he has been to the village before. He was about to be released when a fellow convict asked him to give two one-pound notes to a boy named Pip. This was to be a

repayment for a kindness the boy had done for him. Now, Pip definitely knows that the notes came from his convict (the first convict) in the cemetery near the marshes. The mysterious stranger also relates how Pip's convict was tried again for prison breaking and given life.

Pip is so unnerved by this conversation that he gets off the stage as quickly as it nears his village. He goes to the Blue Boar where he learns that Pumblechook has taken all the credit for Pip's good fortune. Pip goes to Miss Havisham's with the confidence that just as she adopted Estella, she "adopted" him also. He feels that his mission is to be the hero who is "to restore the desolate house, admit the sunshine into the dark rooms, set the clocks a-going...do all the shining deeds of the young knight of romance, and marry the princess."

Pip's romantic attitude is disrupted when he finds that Orlick is now working for Miss Havisham, and it is he who opens the gate for Pip. He goes in to see Miss Havisham, who has not changed in any way and does not, at first, recognize that the beautiful lady sitting beside her is Estella. Pip recognizes her eyes first and then has a fleeting feeling that she resembles someone else, but he does not recognize who.

He and Estella walk together in the overgrown garden, but Pip can only see beauty there because Estella is there with him. They talk of the past, but Estella says she remembers none of the incidences Pip remembers. Estella says, "You must know that I have no heart—if that has anything to do with my memory."

When Pip and Estella rejoin Miss Havisham, Miss Havisham has Pip push her around the bridal table as he did so many times in the past. She draws Pip down to her and says, "Love her, love her, love her...If she favours you, love her. If she wounds you, love her. If she tears your heart to pieces...love her, love her, love her."

Mr. Jaggers arrives; he, Sarah Pocket, Estella, and Pip have dinner together. Miss Havisham does not eat with them. When Pip sees Miss Havisham after dinner she tells him that Estella is to come to London, and Pip is to meet her at the coach and be her escort. This knowledge makes Pip even more sure that he is the gentleman being groomed for Estella. Because he does not want Estella or Miss Havisham to know that he still associates with Joe, he does not even go see him, Biddy, or his sister.

Analysis

Again, Pip's guilt pulls at him, but he ignores its tugs. He knows he should stay at the forge with his "family," but decides against it. In Pip's childhood, he had considered Joe his equal; now Pip regards him as an embarrassment. By this time in Pip's life, he considers himself much better than they.

Pip's snobbish behavior is also recognized with his wanting to take his servant along with him to his little village. He felt it would make quite an impression. But, because Pip is afraid of someone's talking too much, he decides to leave the servant in London.

Dickens uses coincidence again to pull Pip back to his early beginnings. It is a coincidence that he rides on a stage with the two convicts, one of whom is the stranger who had Joe's file and had given Pip two one-pound notes. It is also coincidence that Pip must sit near them and overhear them talking about that very incident in the Three Jolly Bargemen of so long ago. Dickens is a master at weaving his plot intricately through so many characters and having them all in touch with one another in some way.

The nature of love is a prominent theme in Dickens' novel. The reader is shown different kinds of love and asked to decide which is the true love. There is Miss Havisham's definition of love: "It is blind devotion, unquestioning self-humiliation, utter submission, trust and belief against yourself and against the whole world, giving up your whole heart and soul to the smiter—as I did!" There is the simple, uncomplicated, undemanding love of Joe for Pip. And, there is the heart rending, romantic love that Pip feels for Estella. Pip says, "I loved Estella with the love of a man, I loved her simply because I found her irresistible. Once for all; I knew to my sorrow, often and often, against promise, against peace, against hope, against happiness, against all discouragement that could be."

Study Questions

1. Where does Pip stay when he reaches his village?

2. Does Pip go to see Joe, Biddy, and his sister while he is in town?

3. Who rides on the coach with Pip?

4. What does Pip overhear the convicts discussing?

5. When Pip arrives in his village, who does he find has taken all the credit for his good fortune?

6. Who admits Pip into Miss Havisham's gate and is now working for her?

7. How has Estella changed since the last time Pip saw her?

8. What does Miss Havisham tell Pip to do to Estella?

9. How does Pip recognize Estella when he first arrives?

10. Who does Pip envision restoring Satis House to its former glory?

Answers

1. Pip decides to stay at the Blue Boar.

2. No, Pip feels guilty because he does not go see them, but not enough to go.

3. Two convicts ride with Pip on the coach. One of them is the stranger who stirred his drink with Joe's file at the Three Jolly Bargemen.

4. Pip overhears the convict tell the other how he was instructed to give two one-pound notes to a young boy.

5. Pip learns that Mr. Pumblechook has taken all the credit for helping Pip acquire his good fortune.

6. Orlick is now working for Miss Havisham and is the one who admits Pip in the gate.

7. She has become a young woman, even more beautiful than before. However, she is still distant and cool to Pip, but not hateful as before.

8. She tells him to "love her, love her, love her."

9. Pip recognizes Estella's eyes.

10. Pip envisions himself as being the hero who restores the house and marries Estella.

Suggested Essay Questions

1. Discuss the different kinds of love presented in the novel. Give examples to support your essay.

2. Describe how Dickens uses coincidence to piece together his novel, and how do the coincidences affect Pip.

3. How has the relationship between Joe and Pip changed from the beginning of the novel? Explain the reasons for the changes.

Chapters 30 and 31

New Characters:

Clara: *Herbert's fiancee*

Mr. Waldengarver: *a name Mr. Wopsle is using as a stage name*

Summary

While still staying at the Blue Boar, Pip confides to Mr. Jaggers that he does not believe that Orlick is the right man to have a position of trust with Miss Havisham. Mr. Jaggers agrees and assures Pip that it will be taken care of. As Pip walks through the village, most of the people make it a point of seeing him because of his fortunes. However, Trabb's boy ridicules and aggravates him by bowing down to him and then following him down the street crowing at him. Pip catches the stage headed back to London. He sends Joe some codfish and a barrel of oysters because he did not go see him.

Upon returning to Barnard's Inn, Pip finds it hard to keep the Avenger busy. He invents errands for him to do. Pip asks Herbert if he might confide in him. Herbert and Pip sit in front of the fire while Pip talks of his love for Estella. "'Herbert,' said, I, laying my hand upon his knee, 'I love—I adore—Estella.'" Herbert tells Pip that he has known that fact all along. Pip and Herbert both feel that Pip has been chosen for Estella by Miss Havisham. However, Herbert cautions Pip that in the event that this is not the case, he must be able to detach himself from her. Pip assures Herbert that he would never be able to do that.

Herbert then confides to Pip that he is engaged to a girl from London. Her name is Clara, and they plan to be married when Herbert has enough money.

That evening Pip and Herbert go to see a play featuring Mr. Wopsle as one of the actors. After the performance, a man tells the two young men that Mr. Waldengarver would like to see them backstage. Herbert suggests that Mr. Waldengarver is probably Mr. Wopsle. Herbert and Pip visit with Mr. Wopsle and invite him home to supper.

Analysis

Pip's new station in life, one of wealth and prosperity, has grown stronger than his love for Joe. Pip feels guilty for not going to see Joe and seeks to soften his guilt by sending him a present of codfish and a barrel of oysters. Even the present Pip sends is showy and ostentatious and does not indicate any remorse for not wanting to see Joe. He struts through his village feeling extremely proud of himself until Trabb's boy, with his ridicule, reminds him of his past and humiliates him. Back in London, Pip confides to Herbert that he is not sure what his benefactor's expectations are of him. Pip is not even sure if Estella is part of it, but he would be unable to give her up anyway.

Mr. Wopsle's role of Hamlet is a ridiculous farce. The presentation is realistic only in the eyes of Mr. Wopsle.

Study Questions

1. How does Orlick lose his job at Miss Havisham's house?
2. How is Pip treated by the townspeople?
3. How is Pip treated by Trabb's boy?
4. Why does Pip send Joe a gift?
5. What does Pip send Joe?
6. Who does Pip confide in?
7. What does Herbert confide to Pip?

8. What is the name of Herbert's fiancee?

9. When does Herbert plan to marry his fiancee?

10. What play is being performed by Mr. Wopsle?

Answers

1. Pip tells Mr. Jaggers that he does not believe that Orlick should be in a position of trust, and Mr. Jaggers tells Pip that he will fire him.

2. The townspeople want to see Pip, and they treat him with the respect that money brings.

3. Trabb's boy mocks Pip and humiliates him.

4. Pip sends Joe a gift to relieve his guilt for not going to see him.

5. Pip sends Joe codfish and a barrel of oysters.

6. Pip is able to confide in Herbert.

7. Herbert confides to Pip that he is engaged.

8. Herbert's fiancee's name is Clara.

9. Because of their poverty, Herbert and Clara cannot marry until Herbert acquires some money.

10. Mr. Wopsle is acting as Hamlet in Shakespeare's *Hamlet.*

Suggested Essay Topics

1. Discuss the romantic involvements of Herbert and Pip. Which relationship is more realistic?

2. What is a farce, and how is Mr. Wopsle's performance an example of this term?

3. Explain how Pip's love for Joe has changed.

Chapters 32 and 33

New Character:

Colonel: *a soldier condemned to die at Newgate Prison*

Summary

Pip receives a note from Estella telling him that she is to arrive in London, and he is to meet her at the stage. Pip is overjoyed and goes to the coach office hours before her time of arrival. While waiting for Estella, Mr. Wemmick asks Pip if he would like to see Newgate Prison. They go to the prison which Pip finds neglected, disorderly, and depressing. Mr. Wemmick has a knowledge of all the prisoners and speaks with them or tips his hat. Mr. Wemmick introduces Pip to a soldier condemned to be hanged the following Monday. After leaving the prison, Pip feels contaminated by the filth of the prison and its occupants.

Estella arrives and Pip is overjoyed. They discuss Miss Havisham's plans for them. Pip was not only to meet her at the stage but is to send for a carriage and take her to Richmond. Estella is to live in Richmond with a powerful woman who will introduce her into society. Estella tells Pip how much Miss Havisham's relatives hate him, and how she has disliked them all her life. She hates people who deceive and play up to others, as the Pockets do Miss Havisham. Pip sends for tea as they wait for a carriage to take them to Richmond, and Estella inquires about Pip's affairs. When the carriage comes, Pip takes her to Richmond and is told that he may call upon her at any time.

Pip returns to London and goes to see Mr. Pocket. Mr. Pocket is away lecturing on "domestic economy," and Mrs. Pocket is upset because she had given the baby a box of needles to keep it quiet, and there are some needles missing.

Analysis

Pip's relationship with Estella has not changed. She has completely captured his heart, but Pip is still unhappy. He eagerly awaits her arrival in London and anticipates her warm welcome, but she is never warm or overly friendly to him. While they wait for the car-

riage that will take them to Richmond, Estella and Pip have tea together in a private sitting room. Pip states, "I thought that with her I could have been happy there for life. (I was not at all happy there at the time, observe, and I knew it well.)" The happiness that should come with Estella's presence eludes Pip because his affection for Estella is so obviously not reciprocated.

Upon arriving in Richmond, Pip helps Estella move all her boxes into the house. As Pip departs, he stands looking back at the house and thinks, "how happy I should be if I lived there with her, and knowing that I never was happy with her, but always miserable." The relationship is lacking in warmth and love, for there can never be a happy one-sided affair.

Another important influence in Pip's life is Newgate Prison. It seems that criminals, prisons, and lawyers have played a part in Pip's life ever since he was very young and living on the marshes with Joe. After Mr. Wemmick and Pip leave Newgate Prison, Pip thinks "how strange it was that I should be encompassed by all this taint of prison and crime; that, in my childhood out on our lonely marshes on a winter evening, I should have first encountered it; that it should have reappeared on two occasions, starting out like a stain that was faded but not gone; that it should in this new way pervade my fortune and advancement." When Pip leaves Newgate Prison he feels contaminated, but he can never shake off the influence of prisons and convicts throughout his life. Dickens' loathing of the criminal element is due to his association with this atmosphere as a child growing up in London.

Another side of Mr. Wemmick's character is seen as he escorts Pip through Newgate Prison. He seems to be popular with the inmates, and Pip says, "It struck me that Wemmick walked among the prisoners much as a gardener might walk among his plants." After introducing Pip to a soldier who is condemned to die the following Monday, Mr. Wemmick "looked back, and nodded at his dead plant, and then cast his eyes about him in walking out of the yard, as if he were considering what other pot would go best in its place." The prisoners are compared to plants by the use of similes. Mr. Wemmick recognizes that some will die and others will go on to live, much like the plants he cares for in his garden at the Castle.

Study Questions

1. Pip receives a note. Who is it from?

2. Who is coming to London?

3. Where does Mr. Wemmick take Pip?

4. What is Pip's impression of Newgate Prison?

5. What is Mr. Wemmick's relationship with the prisoners?

6. A simile is used to compare Mr. Wemmick in Newgate Prison to something else. What is it?

7. Where is Estella to live?

8. Why is Estella moving to Richmond?

9. How do Miss Havisham's relatives feel about Pip?

10. Mr. Pocket is a lecturer on "domestic economy." Why is this ironic?

Answers

1. The note Pip receives is from Estella.

2. Estella is coming to London the day after tomorrow.

3. Mr. Wemmick takes Pip to Newgate Prison.

4. Pip finds Newgate Prison to be a dirty, dismal, and depressing place.

5. Mr. Wemmick is popular with the prisoners. He speaks with them but maintains an aloofness from them.

6. Mr. Wemmick, walking among the prisoners, is compared to a gardener walking among his plants.

7. Estella is to live in Richmond.

8. Estella is moving to Richmond to live with a lady of high position in order that she may be introduced into society.

9. Miss Havisham's relatives dislike Pip. Estella tells Pip that they "watch you, misrepresent you, write letters about you (anonymous sometimes), and you are the torment and occupation of their lives. You can scarcely realize to yourself

the hatred those people feel for you."

10. Mr. Pocket's lectures on "domestic economy" are ironic because he cannot manage his own children or servants.

Suggested Essay Topics

1. Discuss the influence of prisons, convicts, and criminal lawyers upon Pip's life.

2. Explain why Mr. Wemmick is compared to a gardener in Newgate Prison.

3. Does wealth bring happiness to Pip? Explain this term in Pip's and Estella's relationship.

4. How have Miss Havisham's relatives played a part in Estella's and Pip's lives?

5. Define and discuss the use of similes in these two chapters.

Chapters 34 and 35

Summary

Pip begins to look at the effects of his great expectations, and he does not like what he sees. His wealth has affected others as well as himself. Influenced by Pip's lavish expenditures, Herbert has also spent beyond his means. They join an expensive club called the Finches of the Grove and spend extravagantly. Pip states, "We spent as much money as we could, and got as little for it as people could make up their minds to give us. We were always more or less miserable..." Pip and Herbert sit down and try to straighten out their debts. Humorously, more action is taken in gathering all the debts and papers than in actually paying off any of the expenditures.

A letter from Trabb and Company arrives for Pip telling him of his sister's death. The funeral will be the following Monday at three o'clock in the evening. This is the first time that death has entered into Pip's life, and it causes him to reflect back to his life on the marshes with Joe and his sister. He has no tender remembrances of his sister, but her image seems to be everywhere. He cannot imagine the kitchen without her in it. He thinks of Joe and Biddy and their tenderness and kindness.

He arrives in his village and goes directly to his old home. Trabb and Company has taken over the entire funeral—telling everyone what to wear and where to stand. Refreshments have been set up in the parlour, and Mr. Pumblechook is sampling everything. Pip, Joe, and Biddy follow the body of Mrs. Joe through the village to the cemetery. Joe feels that Mrs. Joe would have liked all the attention; however, he would have preferred to have carried her to the cemetery himself without all the ceremony.

After the funeral, Biddy tells Pip that she will be leaving the forge on the next day and will become the mistress in the new school. Biddy tells Pip that she saw Orlick hiding behind a tree on the night Mrs. Joe died, and that she had just seen him again as they were walking. Pip tells her that he will get Orlick run out of the country. Pip also tells Biddy that he will return often to see her and Joe. Biddy questions Pip and asks him if he really will come often, and Pip is insulted that Biddy doubts him. The next morning Pip leaves to return to London, knowing that he probably will not return, and Biddy was right.

Analysis

Pip's money has not brought happiness. In fact, Pip is becoming more and more unhappy with his circumstances. In spite of having a great deal of wealth, Pip goes farther and farther in debt, dragging Herbert along with him. "My lavish habits led his easy nature into expenses that he could not afford, corrupted the simplicity of his life, and disturbed his peace with anxieties and regrets." Pip wonders if staying home in the marshes and becoming a blacksmith with Joe would have made him happier, but he also realizes that Estella would have haunted him. Pip's unhappiness is confounded when he realizes that his material obsessions are ruining Herbert. Herbert does not have the wealth Pip does, but he tries to keep up with Pip, so interwoven into Pip's unhappiness is his guilt for what he is doing to Herbert. It seems that the farther away from Joe Pip gets, the more unhappy he becomes.

The death of his sister brings Pip back to earth for a while and makes him stop and consider his life now and in the past. The funeral is almost like a mockery of death as Mr. Trabb and Co. hand out mourning clothes for the family and choreograph the funeral procession. Humor is portrayed when Mr. Trabb even decides when the mourners should mourn. "'Pocket-handkerchiefs out, all!' cried Mr. Trabb at this point, in a depressed businesslike voice. 'Pocket-handkerchiefs out! We are ready!'" Joe is probably the only true mourner in the procession. Biddy, with her simple wisdom, knows that Pip will not return to visit Joe.

Study Questions

1. Does Pip's fortune bring him happiness?

2. Pip feels guilty for his part in getting someone in debt. Who is it?

3. Why doesn't Pip pay Herbert's debts?

4. When Herbert and Pip try to straighten out their affairs, what is accomplished?

5. Pip receives a letter from Trabb and Co. What does it say?

6. Why is Biddy going to leave the forge now?

7. What is Biddy going to do to earn a living?

8. Who is still lurking around the forge spying on Biddy?

9. What does Pip promise Biddy?

10. What is Biddy's response to Pip's promise?

Answers

1. Pip's fortune has only brought unhappiness and guilt.

2. Pip feels guilty for getting Herbert in debt.

3. Pip is getting into debt himself, and Herbert would never allow Pip to pay for any of his debts because of pride.

4. Pip and Herbert make a big show of sorting out their bills; however, not much is actually accomplished.

5. The letter from Trabb and Co. states that Mrs. Joe Gargery has died, and the funeral will be the following Monday at three o'clock in the afternoon.

6. Biddy must leave the forge now because it would not be proper for her to stay there with only Joe.

7. Biddy is going to try to get the place of mistress in the new school and teach.

8. Orlick is still lurking around the forge spying on Biddy.

9. Pip promises Biddy that he will return often to see Joe.

10. Biddy does not say anything to Pip's promise. She knows that Pip is only feeling guilt for Joe and that he will not return.

Suggested Essay Topics

1. How has Pip's fortune affected him and those around him?
2. Describe the funeral of Mrs. Joe.
3. Discuss Pip's and Biddy's relationship at this time.

Chapters 36 and 37

New Characters:

Miss Skiffins: *a lady friend of Mr. Wemmick*

Skiffins: *Miss Skiffins' brother who is an accountant and agent; he arranges Herbert's partnership with Clarriker*

Clarriker: *a young merchant that Herbert goes to work for*

Summary

Pip's and Herbert's finances go from bad to worse. Finally, in November Pip "comes of age." On his twenty-first birthday, Mr. Jaggers sends for him. Mr. Jaggers inquires how much Pip is spending, and Pip replies that he does not really know. Mr. Jaggers is not surprised and asks Pip if he has any questions for him. Pip asks if his benefactor is to be made known to him today. Mr. Jaggers answers negatively and reminds Pip of the stipulations given to him when he was a young man living at the forge as a blacksmith.

Mr. Jaggers gives Pip a bank note for 500 pounds and tells him that from now on he is to handle his money affairs entirely by himself. Pip "will draw from Wemmick one hundred and twenty-five pounds per quarter" until the benefactor makes himself or herself known.

Pip wonders if Miss Havisham has confided to Mr. Jaggers the plans for Estella and Pip. Mr. Jaggers makes no mention of Estella or of having any knowledge that Pip and Estella are being prepared for one another. Mr. Jaggers goes to wash his hands, and Pip asks

Wemmick about helping a friend get started in business. Wemmick tells Pip that he might as well throw his money off a bridge as loan it to a friend. Pip asks Wemmick if that would be his opinion at Walworth, and Wemmick replies that "Walworth is one place, and this office is another." As Pip leaves the office he asks Mr. Jaggers to dine with him only out of courtesy. Mr. Jaggers accepts, and Pip thinks how much he would rather dine with Wemmick than with Jaggers. After the dinner, Herbert remarks "that he thought he must have committed a felony and forgotten the details of it, he felt so dejected and guilty." Mr. Jaggers makes people feel very uncomfortable.

The next Sunday Pip goes to Walworth and visits with Wemmick. Wemmick is out walking with Miss Skiffins, and Pip visits with the Aged Parent while waiting. Mr. Wemmick and Miss Skiffins return and cross the drawbridge. Pip and Wemmick go outside to talk in private. Pip asks Wemmick to help him give Herbert a certain amount of money each year and possibly get him a partnership in some business. Mr. Wemmick, impressed that Pip is so generous, tells Pip that Miss Skiffins' brother is an accountant and agent who will help them in this endeavor. They return to the house, have refreshments, and listen to the Aged Parent read the newspaper aloud "for he isn't capable of many pleasures."

Before the week is out, Pip receives a note from Wemmick that a young merchant by the name of Clarriker is looking for intelligent help and, in time, a partner in his business. Herbert is set up to be that help. Clarriker will take Herbert into his business and eventually make him a partner in exchange for 250 pounds and other regular payments from Pip. The transaction between Clarriker and Pip is to be done through Mr. Wemmick and to remain a secret. Excited and happy, Herbert returns to Barnard's Inn and tells Pip all that has transpired. Pip is happy for the first time in a long time knowing that his "expectations had done some good to somebody."

Analysis

Pip anticipates his twenty-first birthday with the hope that his benefactor will make herself or himself known. Instead, Pip is given a set amount of money and will be given a set amount each year until the benefactor sees fit to disclose his identity. Pip decides secretly to set Herbert up in business and seeks the help of Mr. Wemmick. The practical Wemmick who works for Mr. Jaggers will not help Pip in this foolish endeavor; however, the Mr. Wemmick who lives at Walworth patiently listens to Pip's plan and commends him for his generosity. The reader is more aware of the two personalities of Mr. Wemmick after learning of his responses to Pip's request.

Pip's visit to Walworth offers the peacefulness and caring atmosphere that is the opposite extreme from Newgate Prison and Mr. Jaggers. Here Dickens gives the reader a release from unhappiness and hardships and presents a humorous and lighthearted look into Mr. Wemmick's personal life. The reader is introduced to Mr. Wemmick's ungainly lady-friend and watches as he flirts with her. There is contentment and a feeling of well-being in the house. It is almost as if the little drawbridge that spans the small ditch indeed keeps the cares of the world and its realities away from Mr. Wemmick and his family.

It should also be noticed that the only pleasure that Pip has felt in quite a long time is when he successfully and secretly sets Herbert up in business. This act on Pip's part enables him to feel good about himself and shows that Pip's inner goodness has not disappeared entirely.

Study Questions

1. Why does Mr. Jaggers send for Pip?
2. What new financial arrangements are initiated when Pip comes of age?
3. What information does Pip want from Mr. Jaggers?
4. What does Pip want Mr. Wemmick to help him do?
5. Who is going to help with the arrangements for Herbert's future?
6. What does the Aged Parent like to read each night?
7. Who is the shipping merchant who agrees to help Pip with his plan?

8. What device separates Mr. Wemmick from the rest of the world?

9. Who is Mr. Wemmick's lady-friend?

10. How much money did Pip receive on his birthday?

Answers

1. Mr. Jaggers sends for Pip to give him a bank note for 500 pounds.

2. Mr. Jaggers tells Pip that he will receive 500 pounds each year, and he will manage his own business affairs now that he is 21 years of age.

3. Pip is hoping to find out the identity of his benefactor.

4. Pip wants Mr. Wemmick to help him secretly set Herbert up in business.

5. Miss Skiffin's brother is going to help with the arrangements regarding Herbert's future.

6. The Aged Parent likes to read the newspaper aloud each night.

7. The shipping merchant who agrees to help Pip with his plan to help Herbert is Clarriker.

8. A small ditch called a moat separates Mr. Wemmick from the rest of the world. To get over to the Castle, one must cross over the drawbridge.

9. Miss Skiffins is Mr. Wemmick's lady-friend.

10. Pip receives a bank note for 500 pounds.

Suggested Essay Topics

1. Compare and contrast Mr. Wemmick's life in London working for Mr. Jaggers and his life at the Castle in Walworth.

2. Explain the conditions of Pip's financial situation.

3. Discuss the theme, "Does money bring happiness?"

Chapters 38 and 39

New Character:

Mrs. Brandley: *a widow and the lady Estella is living with in Richmond*

Summary

Pip visits Richmond often to see Estella. He is continually hurt by her and states, "I suffered every kind and degree of torture that Estella could cause me." She uses Pip to tease other admirers so he is never happy in her presence, yet he is more miserable when he is not near her. Miss Havisham sends for Estella and instructs Pip to bring her. They arrive at Satis House and Pip notices that nothing has changed. Miss Havisham dotes upon Estella. "She hung upon Estella's beauty, hung upon her words, hung upon her gestures, and sat mumbling her own trembling fingers while she looked at her, as though she were devouring the beautiful creature she had reared."

It is on this visit that Miss Havisham and Estella have their first argument. Miss Havisham is horrified that Estella treats her coldly and without feeling. Estella reminds her that that is how she was reared and replies, "I am what you have made me."

Pip walks in the garden while they argue. When he returns, everything seems to be back to normal, and he and Estella play games as in the past. That night Pip stays at Satis House. It is the first time he has spent the night there, and he is unable to sleep. He gets up and sees Miss Havisham roaming about the house like a ghost.

Pip and Estella return to Richmond, and Pip goes to his club. While at the club, Drummle toasts Estella and Pip is angry. Pip claims that Drummle cannot know Estella and challenges him to bring proof of the acquaintance. The following day Drummle brings a note from Estella proving that they know one another. Pip is devastated. As soon as he can, Pip tries to talk to Estella and warn her that Drummle is not worthy of her attentions. Pip tells her, "I have seen you give him looks and smiles this very night, such as you never give to me." Estella asks Pip if he wants her "to deceive and

entrap" him. She tells Pip that she deceives and entraps all the others except him.

Pip is now 23 years of age and is renting rooms at the Temple in Garden Court. It is eleven o'clock and there is a raging storm outside. He is preparing to put out the light and go to bed when he hears someone on the stairs. Pip goes to the stairs and shines a light for the person coming up the stairs.

The man assending is about 60 years old and dressed like a voyager from the sea. The man keeps trying to take Pip's hands, but Pip tries to keep a distance between them. All of a sudden, Pip recognizes the man as the first convict on the marshes. Pip thinks the man has come to thank him for what he did for him as a child and tells the convict that it is not necessary.

The convict tells Pip that he has worked as a sheep farmer, stock breeder, and other trades in order to make money. The convict asks Pip if his guardian's name starts with a "J" and if he received money when he turned 21. He hints and then tells Pip outright that it was he who has made Pip a gentleman. The convict says, "I'm your second father. You're my son—more to me nor any son. I've put away money, only for you to spend." To this Pip braces himself on the back of a chair and feels that he is suffocating. The convict tells Pip that he has risked his life to come back to London and reveal himself as Pip's benefactor. Pip reels in shock as he realizes that Miss Havisham is not his benefactor and Estella is not destined to be his. He gives the convict Herbert's room to sleep in and closes all the curtains and shutters tightly.

Analysis

This concludes the second stage of Pip's life. The first stage introduces the characters and exposes the central conflicts, and the second stage contains the rising action and adds the complications to the plot. The first stage is referred to as the stage of childhood or innocence. The second stage might be referred to as Pip's adolescence or his sinful state. Pip has left the safety and security of the forge and moved to the sinfulness of the city. The move takes place not only as a physical move for Pip, but also as an inward move within himself. His concerns are now turned toward self-gratification. He seeks to become a different person. He is no longer satisfied with his station in life or his class. This dissatisfaction extends also to his family, and he becomes ashamed of them and of the poor or working class that they represent. Pip is torn between his love for himself and others and his longing for material success. Pip lives in the hopes of Miss Havisham's being his benefactor and the ultimate relationship planned between Estella and himself. It also might be significant that his childhood is spent living within a natural environment—the marshes, the sea, and the wholesomeness of honest working people that bring a simplicity to Pip's life. The next stage of Pip's life is in an environment built and polluted by mankind. It reflects the physical and social complexities of his life. The squalor of London almost rubs off on Pip, and he becomes more and more obsessed with money. He acquires superior feelings towards others.

The convict element has haunted Pip ever since the first chapter of the novel. The recurring theme is presented through coincidences, and Pip is never allowed to forget entirely his first convict. In trying to become upper class, Pip actually associates with lower class characters, which include convicts and the people he sees in Newgate Prison. And now, much to Pip's dismay, he owes his wealth and station in life to a convict.

Miss Havisham, considered upper class by Pip, has met with her first heartbreak since being stood up at the altar. Estella turns from her with proud coldness. The young woman has learned her lessons well. She uses others and intentionally torments Pip with her many admirers. When Pip warns her concerning Drummle, she replies, "Moths, and all sorts of ugly creatures...hover about a lighted candle. Can the candle help it?" It might be considered ironic that a candle represents light and warmth, yet Estella is a cold and dark character.

The stormy night on which the convict returns to see Pip and reveal his identity is a foreshadowing of the information to come. A storm is raging, and the wind has blown out the street lamps and seems to push the smoke back down the chimney. The news that Pip hears is as devastating as the storm outside. It destroys any hopes of his getting Estella. Thoughts of Pip had kept the convict working hard, yet the convict destroys Pip's dreams and crashes him back into reality. Pip states, "But, sharpest and deepest pain of all...was that I had deserted Joe." The convict further complicates Pip's life by staying at his house. Pip realizes that this lower-class citizen is responsible for his good fortune and has spent his life in this endeavor. Estella would never understand or accept this situation.

Study Questions

1. Whom does Pip accompany back to Satis House?

2. When Pip cannot sleep at night, who does he see in the hallways carrying a candle like a ghost?

3. Someone is courting Estella that Pip does not approve of. Who is it?

4. Estella admits that she deceives and entraps every suitor except one. Who is that one?

5. What is the weather like when Pip is visited by his benefactor?

6. Where has the convict been working all this time? What has he been doing?

7. Who is Pip's benefactor?

8. Where does the convict stay for the night?

9. How does Pip feel about the convict staying with him?

10. What will happen to the convict if he is found in London?

Answers

1. Pip accompanies Estella back to Satis House.

2. When Pip awakens at night, he sees Miss Havisham roaming the halls carrying a candle.

3. Pip does not approve of Drummle courting Estella.

4. Estella admits that she does not try to trap or ensnare Pip. She is quite candid with him.

5. When the convict comes to reveal that he is Pip's benefactor, there is a raging storm outside.

6. The convict has been working in Australia as a sheep farmer.

7. The first convict on the marshes is Pip's benefactor.

8. The convict stays in Herbert's room for the night.

9. Pip is frightened of the convict and locks the door leading to his room.

10. The convict had been given a life sentence with the stipulation that he was never to return to London. If he returned, he would be hanged.

Suggested Essay Topics

1. Trace the references to convicts in Pip's life. How have they influenced his life?

2. Discuss the second stage in Pip's life and how it may be called one of sin or adolescence.

3. How does the realization that the convict and not Miss Havisham is his benefactor affect Pip and his expectations.

4. Dickens' characterizations are well known. Describe the character of Estella and her impact upon the novel.

5. Discuss the character of the first convict. Describe his motivations and relate his story while in Australia.

Great Expectations Part III

Chapters 40 and 41

New Character:

Provis, Abel Magwitch: *the assumed name and the real name of the first convict*

Summary

Because Pip has to concentrate on hiding the convict, he pushes his other worries aside for the moment. He decides that he will tell people that his Uncle Provis has come to visit. On the way downstairs to talk to the watchman, Pip trips on a mysterious stranger hiding in the shadows of the stairway who runs immediately. Pip questions the watchman and finds that there were indeed two men who came last night, and the watchman thought they were together. The following morning Pip finds that the convict's real name is Abel Magwitch, and he also finds out the reason why he has come to London jeopardizing his life. Magwitch states, "I've come to the old country fur to see my gentleman spend his money like a gentleman. That'll be my pleasure...If the danger had been fifty times as great, I should ha' come to see you, mind you, just the same." So Pip learns that Provis plans to disguise himself and stay in London.

Pip finds Provis a lodging house in Essex Street at the back of the Temple and rents him a room. Then Pip goes to Mr. Jaggers office to confirm what he has learned from Provis. Mr. Jaggers keeps referring to Provis as "the man in New South Wales." He insists that Pip did not communicate with him but was "informed" of his whereabouts. Pip tells Mr. Jaggers that he thought his benefactor was Miss Havisham. To this, Mr. Jaggers says that Pip never had any evidence to think that. Pip purchases new clothes for Provis, but the more Provis tries on, the more he still looks like a convict. Herbert returns, and Provis makes him swear on the Bible that he will not divulge any information about his whereabouts. Pip is relieved to share the burden with someone and tells Herbert all he knows. Herbert and Pip decide on a plan. First, they must get Provis out of England, and Pip is to go with him in order that he will go agreeably. After they are out of England, Pip is to leave him and have nothing more to do with him.

Analysis

Pip feels responsible for the convict even though he experiences a tremendous aversion to him. He realizes that he cannot accept any more money from the convict, and he is heavily in his debt. The goodness that has been buried inside Pip ever since he moved to London resurfaces as he plots with Herbert to get Provis safely out of London. Pip also realizes that he is professionally prepared for nothing and discusses becoming a sailor. Dickens uses a mysterious stranger again to gain the reader's interest. The dark stranger hiding on the stairs is a source of worry for Pip and for the reader. He does not know if Provis has been followed or if there is another reason for the stranger to be hiding in the dark.

Herbert, Pip's beloved friend, helps him devise a plan to get Provis out of London safely. The two young men are afraid of Provis because of his background; however, they both realize that they know very little of it.

It is ironic that the convict carries a Bible with him and makes Herbert swear on it. Good and evil are again blended. Magwitch takes great pleasure in making a gentleman of Pip. It is probably his only worthwhile accomplishment. The reader does not know what crime the convict has committed, but assumes it must have been a terrible crime to have merited a life sentence.

As Pip helps the convict try on new clothes that will disguise him as a wealthy farmer, Pip states, "To my thinking there was something in him that made it hopeless to attempt to disguise him. The more I dressed him, and the better I dressed him, the more he looked like the slouching fugitive on the marshes." It might be said here that one cannot cover up the past with new appearances. While Pip cannot really change the convict, the reader knows that new clothes and material possessions have not really changed Pip either. Pip's past is always a part of him, and it is his past that has formed him into the young man he is at this time.

Study Questions

1. What is the real name of Pip's convict?

2. What name is the convict traveling under?

3. What is Pip going to tell his acquaintances concerning the convict?

4. Why does the convict return to London?

5. What will happen to the convict if he is found in London?

6. Why does Mr. Jaggers keep referring to Magwitch in New South Wales and Provis who will probably come to London to see Pip?

7. Why is Pip afraid of the convict?

8. Who helps Pip decide what to do with the convict?

9. Who is hiding on the stairs in the dark?

10. Will Pip continue taking money from the convict?

Answers

1. The convict's real name is Abel Magwitch.

2. The convict is traveling under the name of Provis.

3. Pip is going to tell his acquaintances that his Uncle Provis, a wealthy farmer, has come to visit him.

4. The convict has returned to London to lavish more money on Pip and to watch him spend it. The convict wants to en-

joy the only worthy accomplishment he has done in his life.

5. Because the convict had been convicted for life and exiled from London, he must never return. If he is ever found in London, he will be hanged.

6. Mr. Jaggers really knows that Provis is Abel Magwitch; however, if he acknowledges that fact he would have to act on the knowledge that the man is back in London. Being a criminal lawyer, Jaggers would have to have him arrested. In order to sidestep the issue, he refers to Abel Magwitch, the convict, as still residing in New South Wales. The man by the name of Provis is not wanted by the authorities and is free to visit London and Pip.

7. Pip is afraid of the convict because he really does not know anything about the convict's past. He only knows that he must have committed terrible crimes to have been sentenced to life in exile.

8. Herbert helps Pip devise a plan as to what to do with the convict.

9. The mysterious stranger is a mystery for the moment. The unknown stranger adds suspense and intrigue to the plot.

10. Pip tells Herbert that he can no longer accept money from the convict, and he feels that he must repay him for all he has done.

Suggested Essay Topics

1. Discuss the effect of the mysterious man on the stairs.

2. Mr. Jaggers tells Pip that he has no evidence that Miss Havisham was his benefactor. What evidence or indications did Pip have to believe that she was the author of his great expectations.

3. Is it possible to separate oneself from the past? Discuss this theme in relation to Pip and the convict.

4. Discuss the convict's purpose in making Pip a gentleman.

Chapters 42 and 43

New Characters:

Compeyson: *the name of the second convict introduced in Chapter 3; he was Miss Havisham's fiancee who jilted her at the altar*

Arthur: *the name of Miss Havisham's half brother*

Sally: *Compeyson's wife*

Summary

Provis relates his life story to Herbert and Pip. It seems that he has spent all his life in and out of jails. Provis states, "I've been locked up as much as silver tea-kittle, I've been carted here and carted there, and put out of this town and put out of that town, and stuck in the stocks, and whipped and worried and drove." Misfortune has followed him as long as he can remember. He had to rob in order to eat even as a youngster. A soldier taught him to read, and a traveling giant taught him to write. About twenty years ago he was introduced to Compeyson who was "set up fur a gentleman...and had learning. He was a smooth one to talk...and was good-looking too." Provis and Compeyson went into business together. "Compeyson's business was the swindling, handwriting forging, stolen bank-note passing, and such-like. All sorts of traps as Compeyson could set with his head, and keep his own legs out of and get the profits from and let another man in for, was Compeyson's business." While in the association with Compeyson, Provis met another accomplice—a man called Arthur. Compeyson and Arthur had done a "bad thing with a rich lady some years afore, and they'd made a pot of money by it; but Compeyson betted and gamed." Compeyson had lost all the money, and Arthur was dying "poor and with the horrors on him." Arthur was living at Compeyson's house and kept hallucinating that he saw a lady dressed all in white standing in the corner holding a shroud for him.

Arthur died and Compeyson considered it good riddance. Compeyson and Provis were captured and tried for committing a felony—"on a charge of putting stolen notes in circulation—and there was other charges behind." Both men were tried for the same offense; however, Compeyson was given only seven years because he appeared to be a gentleman who had gotten into the wrong crowd. On the other hand, Provis, because of his appearance and his past convictions, received 14 years. Both men were sent to the Hulks where Provis sought an opportunity to kill Compeyson. At one point, he struck Compeyson on the cheek, but he was apprehended before he could do any more damage to him. After the two convicts were captured on the marshes and returned to the Hulks, Provis was put in irons, brought to trial again, and given life.

Herbert and Pip put the pieces together as the convict tells his story, and they realize that Miss Havisham's half brother's name was Arthur. Compeyson must be the man who jilted her. With this new information, Herbert and Pip realize the danger that Provis is in if Compeyson turns informer to permanently get rid of Provis. The need to help Provis get out of the country is more pressing than any of their other problems.

Realizing that he must leave London as soon as possible, Pip goes to see Estella in Richmond and finds that she has gone to Satis House. Pip wonders why he was not asked to accompany her. He decides to go back to the village to see her. When he arrives in the village, he goes to the Blue Boar for breakfast and finds Bentley Drummle there. Drummle makes it clear to Pip that he is to dine with a young lady later, and Pip has no doubt who that might be. Drummle goes horseback riding, and the man who helps him light his cigar looks a lot like Orlick from the back.

Analysis

The convict's story reveals a life of grim struggle. Given little chance for survival, Provis achieves a worthwhile goal in spite of the crimes he has committed and the harshness of his experiences. This gives new insight into the theme of good and evil, for what appears evil (Provis) has certainly produced what appears to be good (Pip's elevation to the rank of gentleman).

Pip is again threatened by the appearance of Bentley Drummle. Pip feels that Drummle is spending too much time with Estella and does not understand their relationship. Dickens tones down their intense and disagreeable meeting at the Blue Boar with humor. Both try to out wait one another in front of the fireplace. There is no doubt that Drummle has the upper hand on Pip and ridicules his village with sarcasm.

Study Questions

1. Who is Compeyson?

2. Who was Arthur?

3. What happened to Arthur?

4. Who did Arthur see shaking a shroud at him?

5. Who was the real mastermind of the crimes committed by Compeyson and Provis?

6. Why does Pip fear Compeyson?

7. Who accompanies Estella back to Satis House?

8. Why does Pip return to the village to see Estella?

9. Who does the man who helps Drummle light his cigar resemble?

10. Why were Compeyson and Provis sentenced differently?

Answers

1. Compeyson is the man who jilted Miss Havisham. He, Arthur, and Provis were partners at one time.

2. Arthur is Miss Havisham's half brother. He and Compeyson swindled her out of all that they could.

3. Guilt has driven Arthur crazy, and he dies at Compeyson's house.

4. Arthur imagines that he sees a woman dressed in white shaking a shroud at him. He knows that when she puts the shroud on him he will die. The woman is Miss Havisham.

5. The real mastermind of the evil plots to swindle and go against the law was the schemer Compeyson.

6. Pip is afraid that Compeyson will turn Provis in to the law.

This would free Compeyson from worrying about Provis, because Provis would still kill him if he got the chance.

7. Bentley Drummle accompanies Estella back to Satis House.

8. Pip realizes the danger that Provis is in and knows that he and Provis must leave the country as soon as possible. Before he leaves, he wants to see Estella.

9. The man helping Drummle resembles Orlick.

10. Compeyson requested that they be tried separately. Compeyson shows up for the trial smartly dressed holding a white handkerchief to his nose. He is an eloquent speaker and blames his erring ways on the influence of Provis. Provis, on the other hand, appears before the court looking ragged and illiterate with a long string of offenses to his name.

Suggested Essay Topics

1. How much influence does a person's appearance have on others? Cite examples from the court trial of Compeyson and Provis.

2. Relate Provis' story concerning his background. Would this knowledge explain why Provis is so intent on making Pip a gentleman?

3. Describe the relationship between Provis and Compeyson.

4. Compare how guilt affects Arthur and how it affects Compeyson.

Chapters 44 and 45

New Character:

Mary Anne: *a young servant working for Mr. Wemmick*

Summary

Pip goes to Satis House to confront Miss Havisham and Estella. He wants to tell them that he knows who the benefactor is and to let Miss Havisham know that it was unkind of her to allow him to think it was she. He states, "I am as unhappy as you can ever have meant me to be." Pip tells her that not all of her relatives are greedy self-seekers. Two of them, Herbert and his father, are honorable and do not deserve to be included with the other Pockets. They have always been honest with Pip and a friend to him. Pip realizes that he will be unable to continue his financial obligations where Herbert is concerned and asks Miss Havisham if she will help Herbert financially without his knowing it.

Pip turns to Estella and admits that he has loved her ever since he first entered Satis House. She does not respond; she just keeps knitting. Pip goes on to tell her of his love and notices Miss Havisham's look of pity for him. Estella answers Pip by saying, "I know what you mean as a form of words, but nothing more. You address nothing in my breast, you touch nothing there. I don't care for what you say at all. I have tried to warn you of this, now, have I not?" Pip now knows for certain that he was not meant for Estella, but he cannot help warning her to beware of Drummle. To Pip's great dismay, Estella confesses that she is going to be married to him.

This news crushes Pip, and he tries to make her see that if he himself cannot have her, she should at least marry someone more worthy than Drummle.

Pip leaves Satis House and walks all the way back to London. As he arrives at the Temple, the watchmen gives him a note. In Wemmick's handwriting is the message, "Don't go home!" Pip finds other lodging for the night, but cannot sleep for worrying about the meaning of the message.

The next morning Pip goes to Walworth to talk with Wemmick. Wemmick tells Pip that Provis' disappearance in New South Wales caused quite a stir. Compeyson is now in London, and Pip's house is probably being watched. When Wemmick heard the news, Pip was at Satis House, so Wemmick went to Herbert, who found another lodging place for Provis. He rents Provis a room in the house where his fiancee lives.

There are three reasons why this arrangement is a good one. One, the house is off the beaten path and not a place where Pip usually goes. Two, the house is near the river, thus providing access to foreign-bound ships when the time comes to get Provis out of the country. Three, Herbert can keep Pip informed about the welfare of Provis since he will be visiting his fiancee in the same house.

Analysis

The confrontation with Estella and Miss Havisham has left Pip feeling desolate and without hope. The news of Estella's impending marriage to someone as unworthy as Drummle devastates Pip. Estella reminds Pip that she never led him on.

The identity of his benefactor has completely changed Pip's life and his expectations. He is now unable to continue his good intentions concerning Herbert and must ask for Miss Havisham's help. Pip is humbled and broken hearted. When he returns and finds the note, all his fears tumble in around him. He worries about Provis, which indicates that there is still good left in Pip.

Wemmick's sincere friendship is demonstrated clearly. He not only warns Pip about not returning home, but also with Herbert's help, safely moved Provis to new lodging.

Dickens' characters may be divided into three groups. There are those who harm others, such as Orlick and Drummle, and there are those who are harmed or hurt, such as Herbert and Pip. The third group consists of those who help others which includes Wemmick, Biddy, and Joe. Wemmick exemplifies the simple honesty and gentleness that pulls Pip to him for help and advice.

The plot begins to become intense as the reader learns that Compeyson is in London, and Provis might be in great danger. Even though he has committed many crimes, the reader feels a sympathy for him because of what he has done for Pip.

Study Questions

1. What favor does Pip ask of Miss Havisham?
2. What confession does Pip make to Estella?
3. Who does Estella plan to marry?
4. Who are the two relatives that Pip ask Miss Havisham not to include with the self-seekers?

5. How does Pip get back to London?

6. What does the night watchman give to Pip, and what does it say?

7. Who has written a warning note to Pip?

8. What two characters are responsible for relocating Provis?

9. Where is Provis now living?

10. What character is in London and threatens the safety of Provis?

Answers

1. Pip asks Miss Havisham if she would secretly supply money for Herbert to remain in Clarriker's employment.

2. Pip confesses that he has loved her since he first went to Satis House.

3. Estella plans to marry Bentley Drummle.

4. Pip asks Miss Havisham not to include Herbert and his father in the group of relatives who are greedy self-seekers.

5. Pip is so unhappy that he walks back to London.

6. The night watchman at the Temple gives Pip a note that says, "Don't go home!"

7. Mr. Wemmick is the one who has written the note.

8. Mr. Wemmick and Herbert are responsible for relocating Provis.

9. Provis is now living in the house where Clara, Herbert's fiancee, lives.

10. Compeyson is in London and threatens Provis' safety.

Suggested Essay Topics

1. Describe the confrontation with Estella and Miss Havisham at Satis House.

2. Discuss the benefits of moving Provis to a room in the same rooming house as Herbert's fiancee.

3. Discuss the friendship that exists between Wemmick and Pip.

Chapters 46 and 47

New Characters:

Mrs. Whimple: *the landlady to the Barleys*

Bill Barley: *Clara's father*

Mr. Campbell: *the name that Provis has taken when he moves into Mrs. Whimple's boarding house*

Summary

Pip goes to Mill Pond Bank to locate the boarding house where Provis is now living. He is greeted at the door by Herbert and meets Clara for the first time. Clara's father lives upstairs; because he is an invalid, he never comes down. Clara's father gets her attention by banging on the floor and yelling. Pip decides not to tell Provis that Compeyson is in London. He only relates the plan that Wemmick has given him. Provis is to stay hidden for awhile, and Pip is not to come see him for fear of being followed. Pip also tells Provis that he must leave the country and that he will go with him.

Herbert comes up with the idea that since the boarding house is right on the river, they take up rowing again. They can go rowing every day so as not to arouse suspicion. Then, when the right time comes, they can row Provis out to sea to board a steamer. As they row past the boarding house Provis is to lower his shade if everything is all right. Pip's entire being is consumed with the fear that he is being watched or followed. He goes to the theater one night where Mr. Wopsle is performing. Pip notices that Mr. Wopsle keeps looking at him from the stage. After the play ends, Pip and Mr. Wopsle meet, and Wopsle says, "I had a ridiculous fancy that he must be with you, Mr. Pip, till I saw that you were quite unconscious of him, sitting behind you there like a ghost." A chill creeps over Pip, and he is afraid to ask who it was that Mr. Wopsle saw.

Mr. Wopsle asks if Pip remembers one Christmas long ago when two convicts had escaped and were found fighting. Pip admits that he does remember, and Mr. Wopsle says, "One of those two prisoners sat behind you to-night. I saw him over your shoulder." Pip realizes it had to be Compeyson, and he immediately sends a written note to Wemmick telling him of the occurrence.

Analysis

Pip's fear that Provis will be found consumes his every move. His concern for Provis reveals the inner character of Pip. He feels responsible for the convict and does not want anything to happen to him. Pip also does not spend any more of Provis' money. He returns Provis' unopened pocketbook and waits as bills and debts begin to pile up. When Pip goes to visit Provis in his new quarters, Provis appears "softer." The reader might wonder if the convict is softer in appearance, or if it is Pip's heart that is becoming softer. Without realizing it, Pip is again changing. He is realizing that goodness comes from within a person, not from external sources like wealth. The boarding house offers safety for Provis for a time, and Pip and Herbert make it a habit to be seen rowing on the river until the time is right to escape with Provis.

Study Questions

1. In whose boarding house if Provis now living?

2. Where is the boarding house located?

3. What is wrong with Clara's father?

4. How often is Pip to go see Provis?

5. How are Pip and Herbert preparing to help Provis escape from London?

6. How is Provis to signal Pip that everything is all right?

7. What name is Provis now going by?

8. Because Pip has no more money, what does he have to do to raise some money?

9. Whom does Pip see at the theater?

10. Who is sitting behind Pip in the theater?

Answers

1. Provis is now staying at Mrs. Whimple's boarding house—the same one as Clara, Herbert's fiancee.

2. The boarding house is located on the river front on Mill Pond Bank.

3. Clara's father is an invalid suffering from gout and too much rum.

4. Pip is not to return to see Provis.

5. Pip and Herbert start rowing every day so that when the day comes to help Provis escape, they will not arouse suspicion

6. Provis' signal that everything is all right is to lower his shade when Pip rows by the house.

7. Provis is now going by the name of Mr. Campbell.

8. Pip would not take Provis' pocketbook filled with money, so now he must sell some of his jewelry in order to pay some of his debts.

9. While at the theater, Pip sees Mr. Wopsle performing.

10. Mr. Wopsle tells Pip that the convict from the marshes was sitting behind him in the theater. That convict was Compeyson.

Suggested Essay Topics

1. Explain how Pip's attitude toward the convict has changed from first meeting him at the Temple.

2. Discuss the plans for helping Provis escape from London.

Chapters 48 and 49

Summary
Pip dines with Mr. Jaggers and Mr. Wemmick. As they dine, Mr. Jaggers tells Pip that Miss Havisham has sent a note requesting that Pip come see her concerning a little matter of business.

Mr. Jaggers brings up the fact that Estella is now married to Drummle and hints that Drummle may be beating her. Mr. Jaggers says, "A fellow like our friend the Spider, either beats, or cringes."

Molly, Jaggers' housekeeper, waits on the table and a movement of her fingers reminds Pip of the way Estella's fingers looked as she sat knitting. Pip notices that "her hands were Estella's hands, and her eyes were Estella's eyes, and if she had reappeared a hundred times I could have been neither more sure nor less sure that my conviction was the truth." Pip is certain that Molly is Estella's mother.

As Pip and Wemmick walk home together, Pip asks Wemmick to relate Molly's story. It seems that she was tried for murder, and Mr. Jaggers got her acquitted. Molly, a married woman with a three year old daughter, had murdered a woman who was much stronger than she in a fit of jealousy. As soon as she was acquitted, Molly went to work for Mr. Jaggers. She became a different person when she started working for Mr. Jaggers, quite tame compared to her previous wildness.

Feeling confident that Estella is Molly's daughter, Pip goes to see Miss Havisham concerning their business arrangement. As Pip enters the room, he feels pity for the woman who shut away the world and who has lost the only person she ever came close to loving—Estella. Miss Havisham says, "I want to pursue that subject you mentioned to me when you were last here, and to show you that I am not all stone. But perhaps you can never believe, now, that there is anything human in my heart?" Pip explains to her his secret history of helping Herbert in Clarriker's business and tells her that it will take 900 pounds to complete the business transaction. Miss Havisham agrees to have Mr. Jaggers give him the money.

Then Miss Havisham tells Pip, "If you can ever write under my name, 'I forgive her,' though ever so long after my broken heart is dust, pray do it!" Miss Havisham kneels at Pip's feet and weeps. Pip assures her that he does forgive her, and she cries, "Oh, what have I done! What have I done."

Pip asks her how Estella came to be her adopted daughter, and Miss Havisham tells her side of the story. Miss Havisham tells Pip that she wanted a little girl to love and bring up and save from experiencing the same fate that she had. She asked Mr. Jaggers to find her a daughter, and one night he arrived with the sleeping child. Miss Havisham named her Estella.

Because Pip feels that he will never return to Satis House, he walks through the brewery and the gardens one last time. While in the brewery, he again imagines he sees Miss Havisham hanging by her neck from a beam. The scene in his mind startles him, and he returns to the house to see Miss Havisham for the last time. As he enters her door, he sees her seated by the fire in her faded and ancient wedding dress. All of a sudden, a coal rolls from the fireplace and catches her dress on fire. She begins shrieking, and Pip throws his coat over her trying to put out the fire that has engulfed her. He pulls the great table cloth from the table and rolls her in it. A doctor is called, and she is laid on the great bridal table. After it is all over, Pip realizes that both his hands are badly burned. Miss Havisham keeps repeating, "Take the pencil and write under my name, 'I forgive her.'"

Analysis

A great change has taken place in the characters of both Pip and Miss Havisham. Both characters regret their previous lives and what they have done to others, for whom they cared very deeply. Pip realizes that his life has been thoughtless and self-seeking. Miss Havisham realizes that she has taken the natural heart from Estella and replaced it with a heart that is cold and unfeeling even towards her. Miss Havisham acknowledges that she has hurt Pip deeply, and the only way she is now able to help Pip is to help his friend Herbert. Pip feels pity for Miss Havisham because she, too, has lost Estella. The pathetic old woman no longer appears as the rich fairy godmother that Pip once saw; she is now only an old woman who shut out the world and allowed herself to be consumed by revenge. Pip feels no hate towards her; rather, he displays a sincere compassion for her safety by risking his own life to save hers.

Dickens uses Pip's knowledge of the criminal histories of Provis and Molly to begin bringing his complicated plots together. Unanswered questions are answered, and the reader discovers that the characters are linked in ways previously unimagined.

In this, the third stage of Pip's life, conflicts are resolved, and Pip reaches adulthood.

Fire has played a symbolic part in the novel. There is the fire at Joe's hearth which is a service to mankind. It is warm and inviting and might be said to represent the character of Joe. It is in that fire that Pip saw Estella's face haunting him when he was a blacksmith working for Joe. On the other hand, there is the small, barely visible fire that burned in Miss Havisham's hearth. It shed no warmth and was of little use. It is this smallness that is seen in the character of Miss Havisham. Even though the fire was small and pitiful, it jumped from its place and destroyed Miss Havisham and badly burned Pip. Dickens is perhaps saying that the small evils in one's life become larger as one grows older and ultimately destroy the person.

Dickens uses repetition for emphasis. Miss Havisham repeats, "What have I done?" over and over. She realizes that her life has been wasted. She keeps repeating, "Take the pencil and write under my name, 'I forgive her.'" It is also ironic that her prophecy comes true. In order for the doctor to treat her, she is laid on the bridal table. The doctor says that her burns are not life-threatening, but the emotional shock is. The doctor has no way of knowing that there is nothing but a shell left of Miss Havisham. The exterior is all that is left, because revenge and hate have eaten away all the inside.

Study Questions

1. Who does Pip believe is Estella's mother? How does he come to this conclusion?

2. How did Mr. Jaggers first meet Molly?

3. What does Miss Havisham agree to do for Pip?

4. How much money will Pip need to complete setting Herbert up in business?

5. When Pip returns to visit Miss Havisham, how has she changed?

6. What three words does she want Pip to write under her name?

7. What happens to Miss Havisham?

8. How is Pip injured?

9. Where is Miss Havisham placed after the fire?

10.   Who brought Estella to Miss Havisham?

Answers

1.   While dining with Mr. Jaggers, Pip recognizes Molly's hands and eyes to be exactly like Estella's. Therefore, after hearing Molly's past, he believes that she is Estella's mother.

2.   Mr. Jaggers was Molly's lawyer. He got her acquitted from a murder case.

3.   Out of remorse, Miss Havisham agrees to help Pip by aiding Herbert in his business.

4.   Nine hundred pounds will make Herbert a partner in Clarriker's business.

5.   Miss Havisham has changed in many ways. She appears almost pitiful sitting in her grave-like house. She begs Pip's forgiveness and realizes that she has destroyed not only her own life, but the lives of Estella and Pip.

6.   Miss Havisham wants the words "I forgive her" written under her name.

7.   Miss Havisham's dress catches on fire and she is badly injured.

8.   Pip's hands are burned while trying to save Miss Havisham.

9.   Miss Havisham is placed on the long bridal table.

10.   Mr. Jaggers brought Estella to Miss Havisham when she was about two or three years of age.

Suggested Essay Topics

1.   Discuss the changes in Miss Havisham, and what has brought about these changes.

2.   Relate Molly's story and how her past is interwoven with Miss Havisham's past even though they never meet.

3.   Trace the changes that have taken place in Pip's character since arriving in London.

Chapters 50 and 51

New Characters:

Mike: *a client of Mr. Jaggers*

Gruffandgrim: *name Herbert uses for Clara's father*

Summary

Herbert takes care of Pip, changing his bandages, and nursing him back to health. Herbert confides to Pip that he cannot marry Clara until her father passes away, because the father requires her constant care.

After two hours of talking, Provis tells Herbert about his marriage. It seems that his wife was a jealous woman and took revenge upon an older and stronger woman because of her interest in him (Provis). She murdered the stronger woman and Mr. Jaggers was her lawyer. On the night that she killed the other woman, she came to Provis and told him that she was going to destroy their child, a little girl. During the trial, Provis did not appear anywhere near the courts for fear that he would be pulled into the proceedings. The lawyer got his wife acquitted for the offense, and he never saw the child again. When Pip helped Provis, Pip was about the same age as his daughter would have been. Pip's kindness touched his heart and reminded the convict of his lost child.

Pip recognizes the story and realizes that Provis is Estella's father. The old convict has no idea that his child lives. Pip goes to Mr. Jaggers to confirm the story and the parentage of Estella. Mr. Jaggers does not want to confirm Pip's hypothesis; however, he puts it to Pip in the form of a nameless case. Mr. Jaggers tells Pip that at one time a client had a child. By pleading that the woman killed her child, and the scratch marks on her hands were that of the child's and not the murdered victims, he was able to get her acquitted.

At the same time, a rich woman wanted a child to adopt. The child was a beautiful little girl, and Mr. Jaggers did what he thought best for the girl. Mr. Jaggers states, "Put the case that he lived in an atmosphere of evil, and that all he saw of children was their being generated in great numbers for certain destruction. Put the case that he often saw children solemnly tried at a criminal bar, where they were held up to be seen; put the case that he habitually knew of their being imprisoned, whipped, transported, neglected, cast out, qualified in all ways for the hangman, and growing up to be hanged." Mr. Jaggers realized that he could altar this child's future for the better and did so. Mr. Jaggers also tells Pip that it might be far better if this information were not shared with the people involved.

Analysis

The discovery of the identity of Estella's parents places more of the puzzle pieces together. One sees the brilliance of Dickens who weaves his master plot through the lives of many characters, connecting them in ingenious ways. Although Mr. Jaggers did not know the identity of Estella's father, he seems to take the information in stride and cautions Pip that it would do no good to tell any of this information to any one of the three people directly involved. The fact that Pip does not want Estella told says a lot for his character. He knows that this information would destroy a woman who has lived in luxury and who believes it to be her total existence. It would also put a darkening cloud over her marriage with Drummle, who is very conscious of appearance and wealth.

These chapters also reveal an insight into London during the nineteenth century. There were no laws or rights for children. Children were at the mercy of the courts or the people in charge. Because Dickens was a newspaper reporter at one time in his career, he was familiar with the extreme punishments handed down by criminal courts. By putting this account of the child and the courts in his novel, he was able to criticize the system.

Study Questions

1. Who takes care of Pip's injuries?
2. What name does Herbert call Clara's father?
3. What did Provis' wife tell him that she was going to do with their child?
4. Who is Estella's father?

5. Where does Pip go to confirm Provis' story?

6. Does Provis know that his daughter is alive?

7. How is the relationship between Pip and Mr. Jaggers different?

8. Will the knowledge of Estella's parents be kept a secret?

9. Why will Pip not tell Estella of the identity of her parents?

10. Who is the client who interrupts the confrontation between Pip and Mr. Jaggers?

Answers

1. Herbert takes care of Pip's injuries.

2. Gruffandgrim is the name Herbert gives to Clara's father.

3. She tells him that she is going to destroy the child.

4. Provis is Estella's father.

5. Pip goes to Mr. Jaggers to confirm the story about Provis, Molly, and Estella.

6. Provis has no idea that his daughter is alive.

7. Pip is no longer afraid or intimidated by Mr. Jaggers. Pip actually knows more about Estella than Mr. Jaggers. Pip has matured, and he is no longer under Mr. Jaggers' rule.

8. Pip and Mr. Jaggers agree that it would do no good to anyone to release any of this information concerning Provis, Estella, and Molly.

9. Estella has married for money, and Drummle is from a wealthy family. The knowledge of Estella's convict father and murdering mother would not be a welcomed fact for the Drummle family. It would destroy her marriage and her life. Pip would never do anything to hurt Estella.

10. Mike is the name of the client who interrupts Pip and Mr. Jaggers.

Suggested Essay Topics

1. Relate Provis' story of his past.

2. Discuss the prison and court system concerning children in nineteenth century London.

3. Research and describe the working conditions for children during the nineteenth century in London. Discuss the child labor laws and how they came about.

Chapters 52 and 53

Summary

With the money supplied by Miss Havisham, Pip takes the check from Mr. Jaggers and goes directly to Miss Skiffins' brother, who in turn takes it to Clarriker. Then the transaction is finished. Clarriker tells Pip that a branch office is needed in the East, and Herbert, in his new partnership capacity, will be in charge of it. Pip says, "I had the great satisfaction of concluding that arrangement. It was the only good thing I had done, and the only completed thing I had done, since I was first apprised of my great expectations."

On Monday Pip receives a letter from Wemmick stating that Wednesday would be the day to do what has been planned for Provis. After reading the letter, Pip is to burn it. Pip discusses the message with Herbert, and they decide that it would be better and safer to ask Startop to help them than to risk hiring a stranger. Pip and Herbert investigate the ships that will be leaving on Wednesday and decide on a steamer headed for Hamburg as the best choice. Because of Pip's burns, he will steer and the other two young men will row. Provis will just sit and watch.

Upon Pip's return from the shipyards, he discovers another letter. This one is dirty and unsigned. It states that Pip is to come tomorrow night at nine to the sluice house by the limekiln located in the marshes. The information that caught Pip's attention was the part that read, "You had better come. If you want information regarding your Uncle Provis, you had much better come and tell no one and lose no time." Pip knows that he would never have gone except for the reference to his Uncle Provis and the fact that the get-away is planned for Wednesday. Nothing must go wrong, so Pip returns to the marsh on the next stage and stops briefly at the inn. The landlord entertains Pip with Pip's own story. The landlord tells how Mr. Pumblechook had been his earliest benefactor and the founder of Pip's fortunes.

Pip travels by foot to the sluice house. Upon entering the small abandoned house, Pip notices a lighted candle on a table, but he sees no one. All of a sudden Pip finds himself encircled with a rope drawing his arms to his sides, causing great pain in his badly burned arm. Then Orlick steps into the light.

Orlick reveals his long-standing hatred for Pip whom he holds responsible for getting him fired from his job at Miss Havisham's house. He felt that Pip had come between him and Biddy.

When Pip asks Orlick what he is going to do with him, Orlick tells him that he is going to take Pip's life. As Orlick sits drinking, he tells Pip how he killed Pip's sister with the abandoned leg iron. Orlick also confesses that he has been watching Pip for some time in order to apprehend him at just the right time. (It was Orlick who was hiding on Pip's stairs that dark and stormy night.) Orlick also knows that Provis is really Magwitch and that he is not Pip's uncle.

As Orlick comes toward Pip with a stone-hammer, Pip begins to struggle and shout. Pip is knocked unconscious as Trabb's boy, Startop, and Herbert rush in. It seems that Pip had accidentally dropped Orlick's letter at the Temple, and Herbert had found it and become worried. Herbert and Startop traveled to the village and asked Trabb's boy to be their guide to the sluice house.

Pip becomes ill after the ordeal with Orlick and is worried that he will not be able to help get Provis out of the country. Wednesday finally arrives, Pip feels better, and at nine o'clock they intend to carry out their plan.

Analysis

Pip has grown to be a self-reliant young man. He has refused further financial assistance from Miss Havisham or from Magwitch. His refusal does not come from a sense of false pride, but from a realization that he has been wrong in the past and needs to mend the mistakes in his life. Even Pip understands that the only good thing he has done since getting his great expectations is to set

Herbert up in business. It was easy to help Herbert when he had great amounts of money; however, it was even more noble when Pip was not receiving any more of Provis' money. It is Pip who refuses to take any more from his benefactor.

When Pip goes to his village and stops at the inn before going to the sluice house, it pulls at his conscience to realize that Uncle Pumblechook has taken all the credit for Pip's good fortune. He remembers that Joe has never said a word. He remarks, " Long-suffering and loving Joe, you never complain. Nor you, sweet-tempered Biddy! I had never been struck at so keenly for my thanklessness to Joe, as through the brazen impostor Pumblechook. The falser he, the truer Joe; the meaner he, the nobler Joe." Maturity has made Pip see Joe as the innocent, humble man that he is.

The conflict between Pip and Orlick is brought to a head when Orlick tries to kill Pip. Orlick is one of the villains of the story who seeks revenge upon the innocent. His vengeance is so planned that he has been watching Pip for a long time. Orlick tells Pip that he is going to put his body into the kiln. Lime dissolves bone as well as flesh, so there will be no trace of Pip's body to be found.

Dickens' use of coincidence helps save Pip from a sure death. Because Pip just happened to drop Orlick's note, Herbert is able to follow him to the marshes and rescue him from certain death.

Pip's illness is partly because of worry and concern over Provis. This concern is genuine; Provis is no longer repugnant to Pip, and Pip recognizes the man as one whose life has dealt him many harsh blows.

Study Questions

1. What two people write Pip a letter in these chapters, and what do they say?

2. What day is Pip planning to help Provis escape?

3. Who is going to help row the boat to the steamer?

4. Where is the steamer going that Pip and Provis are planning to board?

5. At what time was Pip to be at the marshes?

6. Who is taking all the credit for Pip's great expectations?

7. What does Orlick plan to do to Pip?

8. Why does Orlick consider Pip his enemy?

9. Who killed Mrs. Joe?

10. Who rescues Pip from Orlick?

Answers

1. Wemmick writes Pip a letter telling him that Wednesday would be a good day to try to get Provis out of the country. Orlick writes Pip an anonymous letter telling him to come to an old sluice house in the marshes, and he better come in order to get some information about his Uncle Provis.

2. Pip is planning to help Provis escape on Wednesday.

3. Because of Pip's burns, Herbert and Startop will do the rowing.

4. Pip and Provis are planning to board a steamer bound for Hamburg, Germany.

5. The anonymous letter from Orlick instructed Pip to be at the marshes at nine o'clock at night.

6. Uncle Pumblechook is taking all the credit for Pip's great expectations.

7. Orlick is planning to murder Pip.

8. Orlick believes that Pip had him fired from his job at Miss Havisham's house. He also believes that Pip came between him and Biddy.

9. Orlick confesses that he killed Mrs. Joe.

10. Led by Trabb's boy, Herbert and Startop rescue Pip from Orlick.

Suggested Essay Topics

1. Discuss in what ways Pip has changed since finding out that Provis is his benefactor and not Miss Havisham.

2. Describe Orlick's plot to murder Pip.

3. Write a character sketch of Orlick and his part in this novel.

4. Discuss how Pip's feelings for Provis have changed. Why has this happened?

Chapters 54 and 55

New Character:

Jack: *man at the public house where Pip, Provis, Startop, and Herbert stay the night before they try to board the steamer*

Summary

The day has finally come when Pip will try to get Provis out of London to safety. Pip packs only what is necessary because his thoughts are not upon himself but on the welfare of Provis. There are two steamers leaving London on Thursday morning. It is decided that if they miss the first one, they will catch the second.

Pip, Startop, and Herbert begin rowing on Wednesday morning. As they row near Mill Pond Bank, Provis joins them in the boat. The little band of rescuers travel all day and into the night. As night approaches, they find an out-of-the-way public house where they stop for the night. Jack, a dirty and ill-dressed patron of the public house comments that he has seen a four-oared galley going up and down with the tide. This alerts Pip that someone may be following them. The next morning Provis and Pip walk to another area of the beach, and Herbert and Startop pick them up there. They row out to sea, spot the steamer, and begin to position their small boat so as to hail the larger vessel into stopping for the new passengers— Pip and Provis.

As the steamer approaches, the four-oared galley also approaches. There are two sitters in the galley, and one man is heavily wrapped up with his face hidden. The mysterious man points to Provis and says that he is the man. The other sitter in the galley tells Provis that he is under arrest. Provis recognizes the mysterious man as Compeyson, and they lunge for one another, both fall-

ing overboard and capsizing Pip's boat. Provis and Compeyson go under water.

Pip, Startop, and Herbert are pulled aboard; Provis comes to the surface and is rescued. Compeyson drowns. Provis is injured in his chest and suffers a deep cut on the head. Pip tells Provis that "I will never stir from your side…I will be as true to you as you have been to me!"

If convicted, all of Provis' possessions will be forfeited to the Crown. Pip goes directly to Mr. Jaggers who does not offer much hope for Magwitch. Mr. Jaggers tells Pip that since he is not related to Magwitch and Magwitch has no will, Pip will not inherit nor receive any of Magwitch's money or possessions. All that Magwitch has will go to the Crown. Pip decides not to tell Magwitch any of this information, but instead lets him believe that all his money will go to him (Pip).

Herbert tells Pip that he must go to Cairo to run the branch office. He offers Pip a job as clerk in the branch office and invites Pip to live with him and Clara. Pip tells Herbert that he cannot make a decision at the moment because of the situation with Magwitch.

Wemmick comes to see Pip and asks him to come take a walk with him the following Monday. He (Wemmick) has decided to take a holiday on that day. Because of all that Wemmick has done for him, Pip decides to accept the invitation. Pip arrives on Monday, and as he and Wemmick begin their walk towards Camberwell Green, Wemmick picks up a fishing rod. They come upon a church, and Wemmick suggests that they go in. Pip is surprised to find that he is suddenly the best man for Wemmick in his marriage to Miss Skiffins. Aged Parent gives the bride away. As the wedding party leaves to have breakfast together, Wemmick tells Pip that, "This is altogether a Walworth sentiment, please." Pip replies that he understands not to say anything in the vicinity of Jaggers' office.

Analysis

The escape is foiled by Compeyson whose grudge against Magwitch costs him his life. He informed the authorities of the whereabouts of Magwitch and helped identify and apprehend him. This terrible hate has lasted for years and years on both sides.

There is a great change in Pip's feelings for Magwitch. After the capture, Pip takes his place by Magwitch's side and pledges to remain there as long as he lives. "For now my repugnance to him had all melted away, and in the hunted, wounded, shackled creature who held my hand in his, I only saw a man who had meant to be my benefactor, and who had felt affectionately, gratefully, and generously towards me with great constancy through a series of years. I only saw in him a much better man than I had been to Joe." Pip realizes that this crude old man is a warm, loving, and unlucky individual. He realizes that this convict has treated him far better than Pip himself has treated Joe.

Pip is turning from his adolescence, his self-serving quest for his own gain, towards a more mature relationship with others. Pip realizes that he has been shallow and superficial. He begins to renounce some of the values of his London life, returning to deeper and more basic values.

Right after the tense recapture of Magwitch, Dickens lightens the novel with the humorous marriage of Wemmick to Miss Skiffins. Only Dickens can have a character invite another character for a walk and end up with a marriage. Pip becomes a best man without even being asked to attend a wedding. The fact that Wemmick carries a fishing pole is also quite out of the ordinary and humorous. The entire wedding is so nonchalantly planned and accomplished, it helps to relieve the tension built by the escape, capture, and injury of Magwitch. Again, Wemmick makes sure that Pip understands the separation between work and home when he tells Pip that this is "a Walworth sentiment."

Study Questions

1. On what day does Pip, Herbert, and Startop begin their planned escape for Provis?

2. Who alerts the four that a four-oared galley is traveling up and down in front of the public house?

3. On what day do the four meet the steamer?

4. What happens as the steamer approaches?

5. Who is the man in the other galley who is wrapped up in a great coat?

6. What happens to Magwitch?

7. What happens to Compeyson?

8. What will happen to all of Magwitch's money and possessions?

9. Where is Herbert going to work?

10. What position does Herbert offer Pip?

Answers

1. The four young men begin their escape by rowing all day on Wednesday.

2. A man named Jack alerts Pip that he has seen another galley going up and down with the tides in front of the public house.

3. The four young men see the steamer approaching on Thursday.

4. As the steamer approaches, the four-oared galley pulls alongside of Pip and his friends.

5. Compeyson is the other man in the galley. He identifies Magwitch, and they lunge for one another.

6. Magwitch and Compeyson fall overboard together, and Magwitch sustains an injury to his chest and a deep cut on his head.

7. Compeyson drowns during the struggle.

8. Because Magwitch has no will and Pip is not related to him in any way, all of his money and possessions will go to the Crown.

9. Herbert will run the branch office in Cairo.

10. Herbert wants Pip to come to Cairo with him and Clara, and he offers him the job of clerk.

Suggested Essay Topics

1. Describe the escape and capture of Magwitch.

2. Discuss how Dickens uses humor in these chapters.

3. Discuss how Mr. Jaggers is a central figure who ties all the other characters together.

Chapters 56 and 57

Summary

Magwitch lies in prison with two broken ribs which have injured one of his lungs. He breathes with a great deal of pain. Pip sits with him at every opportunity he is given. Pip talks with him, reads to him, and tries to comfort him. "The kind of submission or resignation that he (Magwitch) showed was that of a man who was tired out."

Magwitch's trial comes, and he and 32 other men and women are sentenced together by the judge. They are judged guilty and sentenced to death. Pip begins to write petitions to anyone who might help Magwitch. Appeal after appeal is written and sent on Magwitch's behalf. Pip has become obsessed with trying to find a way to save his benefactor from hanging.

For 10 days, Pip sits with his hand in Magwitch's hand as the convict becomes weaker and weaker. Magwitch says, "You've never deserted me, dear boy." Pip presses his hand and remembers that at one time he had wanted to desert him, but not now. Pip realizes that Magwitch is dying, leans down, and tells him that his daughter is alive, has powerful friends, is very beautiful, and that he (Pip) loves her. Magwitch lifts Pip's hand to his lips, lets it gently sink down upon his breast, and passes away.

Pip returns to the Temple where he becomes extremely ill. He passes in and out of consciousness, but seems to remember someone's coming to arrest him for lack of payment for a jeweler's debt. He also thinks he sees Joe's face in everyone else's face. Finally, Pip asks the person in his room for a drink, and it is really Joe! Pip says, "Oh, Joe, you break my heart! Look angry at me, Joe. Strike me, Joe. Tell me of my ingratitude. Don't be so good to me!"

Joe comforts Pip and tells him that it is the end of May, and the first of June is tomorrow. Pip has been ill about a month. As Pip begins to recover, he asks about Miss Havisham. Joe tells him that she is no longer living and has left most of her wealth to Estella.

Upon Pip's request, she left Matthew Pocket 4,000 pounds and the rest of her relatives very small amounts of money. Joe tells Pip that Orlick is in jail for breaking into Mr. Pumblechook's house.

Finally, Pip is able to go for a ride. Joe carries him downstairs. As they ride, Pip and Joe are both deep in thought. Pip is trying to decide how to tell Joe how he feels about him, because as Pip became stronger, Joe began to become more distant. One morning Pip gets up earlier than usual because he has decided that today he will tell Joe how he feels. Upon going to his room, he finds that Joe has left and gone back to the marshes. Biddy has taught Joe how to write, and he leaves Pip a note telling him of his return. Enclosed in the letter is a receipt for all of Pip's debts, paid for by Joe.

Pip decides to go to the marshes, tell Joe how he feels, and asks Biddy to forgive him and to marry him.

Analysis

Magwitch is resigned to his fate and does not struggle against it. Even the guilty verdict does not seem to upset him. As Pip watches the verdict being given to 32 people, he is incredulous that so many face the same fate. Dickens takes this opportunity to show briefly how different people accept or fight their impending death. Some weep, some sob, some simply walk out of the courtroom as if in a trance. Dickens is giving his readers an insight into the court system of London in the nineteenth century. Dickens felt that society was guilty for the criminals that it made. It is almost as if Dickens is putting society on trial, rather than Magwitch the criminal.

Because Magwitch is so ill, he is allowed to sit during the sentencing. The judge directly addresses Magwitch and singles him out for a special reprimand. The judge lets everyone in the court know that Magwitch is a repeat offender who had been sentenced to life. He tells the public of Magwitch's repeated imprisonments and punishments. Pip sits close to him, holding his hand through all the trial and sentencing. This act on Pip's part illustrates his humility and concern for Magwitch.

The convict is responsible for all the changes within Pip. He is the one who first made Pip feel guilt for stealing. This guilt was the beginning of Pip's loss of innocence. The fact that the convict is Pip's benefactor also bears impressive weight. Because of the new wealth, Pip drastically changes into a self-serving individual who withdraws from those characters who are considered honest, loyal, and true—Joe and Biddy. Then, in the last phase of Pip's life, the convict reverses Pip's downhill decline and causes him to return again to the original goodness within himself.

It is interesting to note that "as I (Pip) became stronger and better, Joe became a little less easy with me. In my weakness and entire dependence on him, the dear fellow had fallen into the old tone, and called me by the old names, the dear 'old Pip, old chap.'" As Pip becomes better, Joe reverts into calling him "Sir." Joe has no idea that Pip is wanting to return to the old relationship with him. Pip has matured. Although Pip feels guilt about the way he has treated Joe, he wants the goodness and innocence to return to their relationship.

Study Questions

1. What injuries did Magwitch sustain when he fell out of the boat?
2. What verdict does the judge pass down to Magwitch?
3. What does Pip do after the judge sentences Magwitch?
4. What does Pip tell Magwitch before he dies?
5. What happens to Pip after the death of Magwitch?
6. Who comes to care for Pip?
7. What has happened to Miss Havisham?
8. What has happened to Orlick?
9. What does Joe leave in his farewell letter to Pip?
10. Who does Pip decide to ask to marry him?

Answers

1. Magwitch broke two ribs and injured his lung, making breathing very painful and difficult.
2. The judge finds Magwitch guilty and sentences him to death

along with 32 others.

3. After the judge sentences Magwitch to death, Pip begins to write petitions on behalf of Magwitch.

4. Before Magwitch dies, Pip tells him that his daughter is alive and that she is beautiful, and he loves her.

5. Because Pip has been spending every spare moment either writing petitions or sitting with Magwitch, he has allowed himself to become run down. He becomes very ill.

6. Joe comes to care for Pip.

7. Joe tells Pip that Miss Havisham has died.

8. Joe tells Pip that Orlick is in the county jail for breaking into Mr. Pumblechook's house and assaulting him.

9. Joe has paid all of Pip's debts and left the receipt in his farewell letter.

10 Pip has decided to ask Biddy to forgive him for his past actions and to marry him.

Suggested Essay Topics

1. Research and discuss the court system in London during the nineteenth century.

2. Describe the last days between Pip and Magwitch.

3. Discuss the many ways that Magwitch has influenced and changed Pip's life.

4. Explain why Joe becomes more distant as Pip becomes healthier.

Chapters 58 and 59

New Characters:

William: *a waiter at the Blue Boar*

Georgiana M'ria: *Mrs. Joe's given name*

Squires: *the landlord of the Blue Boar*

Summary

Pip returns to his village and goes to the Blue Boar where he finds that the people treat him more coolly now that he has no fortunes. He takes a walk to Satis House and finds that it is being sold as old building material, the furniture to be auctioned off. When he returns to the Blue Boar, he encounters Mr. Pumblechook who instructs him to tell Joe that he (Pip) has seen his original benefactor. Pip is incredulous, telling Pumblechook that he does not see his benefactor here at all. Pumblechook calls everyone's attention to Pip's ingratitude and elevates himself by making it known that he would do "it" all again though Pip continues to prove ungrateful.

Pip goes to the school house hoping to see Biddy at her work, but the school is closed. He proceeds to the forge expecting to see the fires of the forge and Joe hard at work. The forge is also closed. As Pip draws nearer his childhood home, he sees Biddy and Joe standing outside the cottage. When they see Pip approaching, Biddy weeps and runs into Pip's arms. Bursting with happiness at seeing Pip, Biddy tells him that she and Joe were married that day. Pip is glad that he did not disclose his plans concerning Biddy to Joe when he was ill in London.

Pip tells Joe and Biddy that he owes them so much more than just money. He promises to repay Joe for the money that he spent paying his debts in London. He begs their forgiveness for the way he has acted and says, "Pray tell me, both, that you forgive me. Pray let me hear you say the words, that I may carry the sound of them away with me, and then I shall be able to believe that you can trust me, and think better of me, in the time to come!"

Pip sells all that he has and goes to Cairo to become a clerk for Clarriker. He repays his debts, lives with Herbert and Clara who are now married, and eventually becomes a partner in the business. Clarriker reveals Pip's secret concerning Herbert's partnership. The business does well, and Pip stays in contact with Joe and Biddy. Pip stays away from London for 11 years. Then one day he returns to the forge to find the same graying Joe seated by the fireplace and a little boy who looks just like Pip sitting beside Joe. The little boy has been named "Pip," and Joe and Biddy also have a little girl.

Biddy asks Pip if he is over Estella. He answers that he is, but deep within him, he wonders. He has heard that Drummle was cruel to her and that they separated. Drummle was also cruel to his horses, and it was that cruelty that cost him his life. Pip returns to the site of Satis House and finds Estella there, walking in what was once the garden. Abuse and heartache have softened Estella, and she says, "I have been bent and broken—I hope—into a better shape."

The original ending states that after Drummle was killed, Estella married a Shropshire doctor, and they lived modestly on her wealth. In the original ending, Estella and Pip do not regain their relationship; whereas, in the more popular version, it is implied that they will never part from one another again.

Analysis

The novel has two endings, the original unpopular one and the second one that proved more acceptable to Dickens' readers. Probably the original ending was more realistic, but the public wanted the relationship of Pip and Estella to have another chance after both had changed so drastically.

All the mysteries have been solved at the close of the novel. Pip, whose beginnings were humble and noble on the marshes, becomes at the end of the story, the same decent person he was at the beginning. The first stage of the novel, Pip's childhood, is filled with satisfaction, loyalty to Joe, and contentment with his social class position. In the second phase of the novel, he becomes dissatisfied and sets high goals for himself after being affected by the appearance of Estella and Miss Havisham in his life. The internal conflict begins at this stage of Pip's life. The first stage represents the down-to-earth simplicity of Pip's childhood, and the second stage reflects the sinful era of his life when he turns away from all that he knows is good and honorable.

The busy industrial life in London reflects the emotional turmoil within Pip's life. The serenity of the marshes is replaced with crowded streets, Newgate Prison, and complexities brought about by indebtedness, overspending, and the identity of his real benefactor. Pip suffers socially and physically.

The third part of the novel represents the redemption. Pip turns from his sinful and thoughtless ways and returns to his beginnings. In the last chapters of the book, as Pip draws closer and closer to Biddy and Joe, he has "a sense of increasing relief as I (Pip) drew nearer to them, and a sense of leaving arrogance and untruthfulness further and further behind." Pip realizes that wealth and happiness do not necessarily go hand in hand. He learns that life is made up of unexpected turns and events all of which form the individual into the person he will become.

Guilt for doing wrong has affected Pip's life from the very beginning of the novel. Good and evil and their effects upon his life have helped shape his life and have caused him to return to his humble beginnings. While he does not return to the marshes to become a blacksmith, he does return spiritually and emotionally to the values he learned there. Also, the effects of wealth are closely associated with goodness and evil. It might be noted that while Magwitch was a criminal and considered to be evil, the money that he gave to Pip was gained through honest work and the unselfish desire to make Pip into something that Magwitch could never be. Miss Havisham, on the other hand, had wealth, but never had happiness. She too tried to reshape another individual.

While changes take place within several of the characters, Pip is the one who changes the most. The novel has been labeled as a *bildungsroman*, which means a "novel of changing or education." Pip's changing comes about as a result of education or spiritual growth. How Pip resolves the conflicts within his life is the central focus of the novel.

Study Questions

1. When Pip returns to his village and the Blue Boar, how do the townspeople treat him?

2. What is happening to Satis House?

3. Who still believes that he is the original benefactor for Pip's fortunes?

4. Pip returns on a very special day in the lives of Biddy and Joe. What is it?

5. What does Pip beg Joe and Biddy to do?

6. Where does Pip go after leaving Joe and Biddy?

7. How many years did Pip stay away from London before returning again?

8. When Pip returns to see Joe and Biddy, what new additions have occurred in their family?

9. What has happened to Estella?

10. Pip goes to look at the place where Satis House once was, and who does he find walking there?

Answers

1. The people in Pip's village have heard of his loss of fortune and treat him coolly.

2. Satis House is being torn down for building materials, and the contents are being sold at auction.

3. Mr. Pumblechook still believes that he is the original benefactor.

4. Pip returns on Biddy and Joe's wedding day.

5. Pip begs Joe and Biddy to forgive him.

6. After leaving Joe and Biddy, Pip goes to Cairo to join Herbert and Clara and work there as a clerk.

7. Pip remains in Cairo for 11 years before returning to his village.

8. Joe and Biddy have a daughter and a son named Pip.

9. Estella has been treated cruelly by Drummle, and they have separated. Drummle has been killed by his horse as a result of his cruelty to it.

10. Pip returns to the site of Satis House and finds Estella walking in what once was the garden.

Suggested Essay Topics

1. Describe the two endings of the novel. Which one do you

prefer and why?

2.   Discuss the idea or theme that money brings happiness. Cite examples from the novel to support your opinion.

3.   How has guilt affected Pip's life?

4.   Explain why the love between Joe and Biddy is the only true love in the novel.

Sample Analytical Paper Topics

Topic #1

Pip's life is influenced by several characters in Dickens' *Great Expectations*. Some of these influences affected Pip in a positive way; others were negative. Write an essay analyzing the characters who played an important role in Pip's life both in a positive and negative way.

Outline

I. Thesis Statement: *The role of Pip in* Great Expectations *is developed through the positive and negative influences of Joe, Abel Magwitch, and Miss Havisham.*

II. Influences of Joe

    A. Positive influence

        1. Exhibits honesty

        2. Gives Pip's early life stability

        3. Gives Pip unconditional love

        4. Possesses a forgiving nature

        5. Exemplifies the goodness of hard work

    B. Negative influence

        1. Represents the lower class

      2.   Is a source of embarrassment to Pip

III. Influences of Abel Magwitch

    A. Positive influences

        1.   Forces Pip to recognize what is really important in his life

        2.   Provides the means for Pip to become a gentleman

        3.   Loves him unconditionally

    B. Negative influences

        1.   Tries to mold Pip into a caricature of the upper class

        2.   Represents the lower class and criminal element

        3.   Provides the money which will result in Pip's downfall

IV. Influences of Miss Havisham

    A. Positive influences

        1.   Helps Herbert at the request of Pip

        2.   Enables Pip to see that wealth does not bring happiness

    B. Negative influences

        1.   Manipulates people

        2.   Tries to mold Estella who ultimately hurts Pip

        3.   Makes Pip unhappy with his station in life

V.   Conclusion: Joe, Miss Havisham, and Abel Magwitch are three major characters in Dickens' novel who have influenced and developed the role of Pip.

Topic #2

   Great Expectations is a portrait gallery of many characters. These characters are interwoven throughout the novel in a masterful way. Write an essay illustrating how suspense and coincidence help tie these characters together and create an exciting novel for the reader.

Outline

I.   Thesis Statement: *The use of suspense and coincidence helps Dickens create not only a spellbinding novel to read, but an array of characters whose lives are interwoven one with another.*

II. Coincidence

    A.   Enables characters to be tied together

        1.   Magwitch knew and was associated with Miss Havisham's fiancee

        2.   Molly is Estella's mother

        3.   Magwitch is Estella's father and Pip's benefactor

        4.   Pip loves Estella and she is Magwitch's daughter

        5.   Mr. Jaggers is Miss Havisham's and Abel Magwitch's lawyer

    B.   Promotes the plot

        1.   Pip finds Magwitch in the cemetery and helps him

        2.   Pip meets and falls in love with Magwitch's daughter at Miss Havisham's house

        3.   Pip receives his fortunes after his many visits with Miss Havisham

        4.   Pip accidentally drops the note from Orlick

III. Suspense

    A.   Creates interest for the readers

        1.   Pip does not really know the identity of his benefactor until the end of the second stage

        2.   Convicts seem to be a part of Pip's life from the beginning of the novel

    B.   Supplies information in bits and pieces

        1.   The convicts at the beginning of the novel do not have names

        2.   A mysterious stranger stirs his drink with Joe's file

   3. Pip passes an unidentified gentleman on Miss
       Havisham's stairs

   4. Pip stumbles over someone on his stairs at the Temple
       on a stormy night

   5. The pale young gentleman at Miss Havisham's house
       is Herbert

   6. The past of Magwitch, Miss Havisham, and Estella is
       revealed by key characters

IV. Conclusion: The novel is made more interesting to read be-
    cause of its vast number of characters tied together through
    the art of suspense and coincidence.

Topic #3

Humor is used in a novel for many reasons. Write an essay
showing how humor is used in *Great Expectations* to entertain and
to relieve the tension brought about by frightening or intense actions in the novel.

Outline

I.   Thesis Statement: *In the novel, Dickens uses humor to relieve
     the tension built by intense moments and to provide entertain-
     ment for the reader.*

II. Relieves the tension built by intense moments in the novel

     A. Pip's encounter with the first convict in the cemetery

     B. Mrs. Joe's funeral

     C. Mr. Wopsle's career as an actor

III. Provides entertainment for the reader

     A. Joe's visit to Pip in London

     B. Wemmick's home life with the Aged Parent

     C. Wemmick's wedding

     D. Wemmick's courtship of Miss Skiffins

     E. Trabb's boy's ridicule of Pip when he returns to the village

F.   The Christmas dinner when Pip was young

G.   Pip's fight with the pale young gentleman

IV.   Conclusion: Tension is relieved and entertainment is provided for the reader through Dickens' use of humor throughout his novel.

Topic #4

Pip's life can be divided into three phases or stages. Write an essay explaining the three stages of Pip's development.

Outline

I.   Thesis Statement: *Pip's development can be divided into a stage of innocence, a stage of sin, and a stage of redemption.*

II.   The stage of innocence

A.   Pip's life with Joe at the forge

B.   Pip's encounter with the convict on the marshes

C.   Pip's introduction to Miss Havisham and Estella

D.   Pip's relationship with Biddy

III.   The stage of sin

A.   Pip's life in London

1.   Pip's desire for material possessions and signs of wealth

2.   Pip's social snobbery

B.   Pip's relationship with Joe and his past

IV.   The stage of redemption

A.   Pip's relationship with Magwitch

B.   Pip helps set Herbert up in business

C.   Regards Joe and the marshes more favorably

D.   Pip's new relationship with Miss Havisham and Estella

V.   Conclusion: The three stages in Pip's life helped to mold his character and to help him develop into maturity.

SECTION SIX

Bibliography

Dickens, Charles. *Great Expectations.* New York: New American Library, 1963.

Harvey, Sir Paul, Ed. *The Oxford Companion to English Literature.* Oxford: Clarendon Press, 1967.

Prentice Hall Literature: Gold. New Jersey: Prentice Hall, Inc., 1989.

Steward, Joyce Stribling, and Virginia Rutledge Taylor, eds. *Adventures In Reading: Classic Edition.* New York: Harcourt Brace Jovanovich, 1968.